EAT THE ELEPHANT

How to Write (and Finish!) Your Novel One
Bite at a Time

JEN CROSSWHITE

To my students, who were the best guinea pigs as I was working out this material.

A writer is a world trapped in a person.

Victor Hugo

Introduction

In 2003, I stood in a hotel room in Houston, wondering if I had made a complete mistake by coming to this writer's conference. I didn't know anyone; I had a two-year-old and five-year-old at home. Downstairs, when I had peeked in the conference room after registering, the rapid chatter of voices made it seem like everyone already knew each other. I wanted to run back and hide in my hotel room the whole four days.

But the trip had been expensive. And I had a book I had been writing. Finding time to write was hard with two little ones. Was it what I was supposed to be doing?

I had always wanted to be an author. The book I'd been working on started as a high school AP English project. It had been a whole 100 pages and transported my class back in time to 1881 Oregon. Now, nothing about that original story remained, other than the setting and a few characters' names. Since then, I'd learned a lot more about writing and put it in to practice. It was time to see if it had been wasted time.

I left my hotel room and continued through the conference. I met some other writers in the same boat I was: knowing no one and feeling alone. I attended my appointment with an editor from my dream publishing house. She liked my story and wanted to see more of it. And another appointment garnered me a potential agent.

That seemed like confirmation I was supposed to write.

I arrived home with renewed desire to write and improve my craft. Those writers I met? They became critique partners and life-long friends. I was blessed doing what I loved with good friends along the journey.

And yet, my book didn't get published. It would take several more years before I truly landed an agent. I kept coming close, but no publishing house would give me that coveted contract.

I kept writing. I kept going to writer's conferences. I kept learning. I wrote other books.

Then I went through a divorce and became a single mom struggling with two special needs children and how to put food on the table. And writing slowly gave way to survival. For nine long years I wondered how I had come so far just to have it come to nothing. I put my hopes and dreams on a shelf and wondered.

Then a Harper Collins imprint hired me as a managing editor. Most of my previous experience in publishing had been from the author's point of view. Now I had a chance to see what it was like from the other side. I learned every aspect of publishing.

And I was shocked.

Writers received relatively little compensation and were locked into contracts that gave them no control over their work. In addition, our publishing pipeline was so full, we were booking writers three to five years out. When I sat on publication board meetings, where we decided which books we were going to publish, I saw books turned down most often for reasons that had nothing to do with the quality of writing: one of the booksellers didn't like the subject or the title was too similar to something we had just done.

When some of my author friends started talking about self-publishing, I took notice. They started talking numbers, and I knew they were making more money than traditionally published authors. I had enough experience on both sides of the publishing desk that I knew what it took to put out a quality book. I jumped in with both feet.

I released my first book, *Coming Home*, in November 2016. Because I had two others nearly finished I was able to get them out relatively quickly as well. But then I got stuck. Those books had been workshopped, edited, critiqued over many years. How could I make sure my next books were as good? How could I put books out faster? And make sure that everything I'd learned about writing went into my next books?

For over fifteen years, I had been working with writers of all skill levels, from beginners to bestselling, multi-published authors, as an editor and coach, helping them make their stories better. I started to see patterns, recurring things that were present in good writing and missing in beginning writing.

Not only did I find some of the same pitfalls, I found that writers got bogged down in the creation of the novel itself. There are a lot of books on individual aspects of writing, but how do you translate that to your own work? How do you know if you are applying it correctly? Creating a novel is a huge undertaking. How do you juggle the forest and the trees?

The Novel Blueprint

One day, I finally took a huge roll of butcher paper and rolled it across my dining room table and started charting everything someone would need to know about writing a novel. It took about a week! But what I came up with was the Novel Blueprint.

I shared my Novel Blueprint over a video chat with my published author friends, all of whom were bestselling authors. There were a lot of "aha!" moments. And "I need to go back and fix that" and "This inspires me to work on my next book."

After having shared this method with many writers at every level of writing skills, what I've discovered is that the Novel Blueprint addresses these common problems.

- Each time I write a book it feels like I'm starting from scratch. How do I write a book without reinventing the wheel each time?
- There are so many pieces to juggle. Where do I even begin?
- I can't finish a book. I get partway through and then I get stuck.
- How do I write faster and better?
- There's a lot to remember about writing a book. How do I make sure I hit all the important things?
- How do I write a book that readers rave about and tell their friends to buy?

Pantser or Plotter? Or Blueprinter?

In the novel writing world, it's not unusual to be asked, "Are you a plotter or a pantser?" In other words, do you plot out your book with a detailed plan or do you write by the seat of your pants, also known as a discovery writer. The novel blueprint eliminates the dichotomy in the writing world between plotting and pantsing.

Each has pros and cons. With pantsing, you discover the book as you write it. It harnesses the fun of creating, but it keeps the writing at the "trees" level. The writer doesn't have a clear picture of where the book is going or even who the characters are before beginning to write. It often involves a lot of rewriting or tossing out a book and starting over because the plot is not strong enough to sustain a whole book or the author has written themselves into a corner. Can you imagine writing a whole novel, just to have to scratch it and start over? Joshilyn Jackson (one of my favorite authors) did that.

With plotting you get a good overview of the whole book and its arcs by laying out each scene, often in intricate detail. This is a much more "forest" level view, but this often removes the joy of the creative process. Many writers would rather poke their eyes out than plot out their whole book in advance.

So I coined the term blueprinting. Just as you would not build a house without a detailed set of blueprints, you shouldn't write a novel without one. The Novel Blueprint gives you all the important elements such as foundation, walls, and windows, but leaves the fun creative parts intact, much like furnishing a room and picking out paint colors.

If you started building a house like a pantser, you would build the living room and decorate it before moving on to decide what other rooms your house might need. But what if you forgot to include a window or a hallway? Now you have to demo a beautifully painted wall. Ouch. Much like cutting a beautiful scene that doesn't work with the overall story.

If you built a house like a plotter, you'd have all the furniture arranged, all the finishes and paint colors picked out before you even broke ground. Which makes the process actually take longer and can rigidly confine you to a schedule when the unexpected happens.

The Novel Blueprint method gives you all the major components you need to construct your novel while still allowing for the element of surprise and the joy of creativity. It helps you write faster because you won't have to be rewriting and deleting. When you sit down to write, you'll know what you're going to write.

It will help you write a better book, rich with characters that are believable and story arcs that are compelling.

And it gives you a method you can use on book after book so you know exactly what you need to do each time you sit down to write.

It took me thirteen years to get my book published. In the traditional world, that's not a terribly long time to wait to get your book published. But there is a better way to shortcut the process. Let me show you how, from my experience on both sides of the publishing desk, saving you time and money. Don't wait thirteen years to see your book in print. Start the journey today.

How do you write a book? The same way you eat an elephant: One bite at a time.

Let's eat!

A Note Before Starting

To be a good writer you need craft and content. That is, you need to have a good idea and know how to execute it well. Without both of these components, your work won't get the attention you would like, either from traditional publishers or from readers if you indie publish.

It takes a long time to master the craft of writing well enough to sell a book. Malcom Gladwell in his book *Outliers* says it takes about 10,000 hours to become an expert at something. I don't think writing is an exception.

This is to encourage you, not discourage you. Know up front that it will take time, and consider it like learning any new skill. You may stink at the beginning, but you will get better with practice and continuing education.

There are several ways to do this.

Join a critique group

Not all groups are created equal. But regularly sharing your work with others and getting feedback is invaluable. And you also learn as you read and critique others. Plus, the camaraderie of being with other writers who "get you" helps provide emotional strength through those tough times. They understand because they've been there too.

Even if you can't find a critique group, you can often find likeminded folks online or in person. I run a membership group for writers that, while it doesn't provide critiques, does provide that kind of camaraderie and accountability you can find in a traditional critique group. For more information, see the Resources section in the back of the book.

Write regularly

Regularly can mean different things to different people, but you can't maintain your craft if you don't practice it regularly. Think of any kind of talent, skill, or feat. They all require regular practice to maintain peak acuity. Writing is no different.

Go to conferences

Critique groups are a great way to interact with other authors. But at conferences you can meet new people, learn new craft techniques, get critiques, and meet with industry professionals. It can be just the shot in the arm that your writing life needs.

Keep learning

Read books, attend conferences, take classes. All of these will help you in some way or another become a better writer. There is a saying that leaders are learners. Well writers are learners too. Never stop trying to learn and perfect your craft. See the Resources section for more about the classes I teach.

Get professional help

You will get to a point where you need more than what your critique group or classes can provide you. You need someone who can give you their professional opinion of your work and help you improve your strengths and manage your weaknesses. That's when it's time to hire an editor. See the Resources section for more information on how to find an editor.

Separate writing and editing

Writing and editing are two different parts of the brain. One of the biggest causes of writer's block is mixing up the editing and writing brain. While you are setting up the Novel Blueprint, you might find yourself more in Editing or Analysis brain. Resist the urge to critique or change any actual writing at this point. You want to stay in Creative or Writing brain to keep the ideas flowing. Jot things down now. Fix things later. I use the Document Notes section of Scrivener to keep track of these types of things so I can keep writing. Whatever method you use, create a place to put those niggling thoughts so your creative brain can get back to creating without interference.

When you are done Creating, put your work aside and come back to it later. A little distance is a great thing. I usually start each writing session reading over what I wrote last time, making changes to satisfy my Editor brain. I've had usually a day's break from the writing, so I can see things a bit more clearly. Now I can come back with the Editor brain and start applying structure and analyze and fix things.

Then when I get into my new writing, my Editor brain is satisfied that the system works and nothing will be forgotten. The process of turning off your Editor takes a bit of training, but your brain can get better at it with time. Just keep reminding yourself that you can fix it later. Even if you literally write those words in your manuscript.

Remember your why

Michael Hyatt is fond of saying, "Go back to the why." Whenever you get discourage or don't know what to do or want to give up, go back to *why* you are doing what you are doing. Why are you writing? To teach, encourage, persuade, comfort, entertain, impart some spiritual truth, share a journey? There's no right answer here. But spend some time thinking about your reasons to write. Because during the dark times (and they will come) your *why* will keep you pressing on.

What does success look like for you? There is no right or wrong answer for these questions, and it can sometimes take awhile to tease out the answers. But the answers will determine the steps you take in your writing career.

Maybe you just have a burning desire to write this story. It could be something that has haunted you for years and you just need to write it. You want to see it in print and tell all those people that keep asking about your book that it's finally done and they can buy it online! You might have ideas for other books, but they're not as strong as this one. It's perfectly fine to write one book.

Maybe in your stage of life, you don't have a ton of time. The idea of writing a book every six months is about equal to climbing Mount Everest. There just aren't enough hours in the day or energy left over to make writing a top priority. And that is perfectly fine. Learn what you can. Make steady progress where you can. Carve out time here and there and get ready and prepped with all you need so that when you do have time, you know how to make good use of it.

You might be at a place where you want to make writing your career. You know there's a cost to it. A financial cost, the cost of your time, what you have to give up to fit in writing. But it is important to you. At this stage, you want to know about the business aspects of writing as well as the actual writing. Email lists, ads, marketing, launching, and all of that will be on your plate as well.

Any of these choices or any other version of them are all perfectly fine and legitimate choices. But they do have different paths. They all include the foundation of good writing and developing your craft. But after that, they diverge into how much marketing, newsletter, ad, and business-type things you want to learn or become knowledgeable about. That's all beyond the scope of this book, but there is a ton of information out there as well. My favorites are in the Resources section of the book.

Each of these paths have a different game plan and a different way of spending your time and money. So it's important to spend some time on your "why" for writing before you discover you're headed down the wrong path. Some people just want to write books, don't particularly care if they make a living at it, but really don't want to do the marketing and business side of it. And that's fine.

The problem comes when they start comparing themselves to those who are making it a business, and then they feel like they're doing something wrong because that's not what they are doing. So when you are clear on your particular path, you can get the info you need and not compare yourself to anyone else's journey. There's enough difficulty on this journey without feeling like yours has to be like someone else's. You get to define what success looks like to you. No one else.

Terminology

There are a lot of different ways to refer to parts of the story craft. Different authors on craft will choose different terms. Some don't like the term hero because it implies only male characters. They prefer the term lead or main character or protagonist. Sometimes the villain will be called the antagonist (not to be confused with the anti-hero, which is actually a hero type).

I mostly use the term hero because it's shortest to type! Also, I write romance, and it is just easier to use hero/heroine to talk about both lead characters. When I'm using the word hero alone, I am referring to either a male or female main character. There's no right or wrong way, so just use what works for you.

The Novel Blueprint

(For a downloadable PDF version, visit http://www.
tandemservicesink.com/wp-content/uploads/2019/09/Story-
Blueprint-2.pdf)

Nugget

What if?

- Whose story is it?
- What's happening?
- What's at stake?
- What's the theme?

Do it

- One-paragraph summary (first two steps of the
  Snowflake advancedfictionwriting.com/articles/
  snowflake-method/)
- One sentence to set the story up

- Hints at the lie she believes and the ensuing conflict
- One sentence for each of the three main disasters in the story
- One sentence for the ending.
- Include theme, internal issue, plot issue
- For character use noun (skill, trait, competency) + adjective (emotional state)

Example

She's an anxious-to-be-accepted schoolteacher returning to her suitor to set her plan in motion to find her place in proper society, as if her past never existed. But when a stack of money shows up in her bag, she thinks her past that she has desperately tried to hide has come back to haunt her, putting all her plans in jeopardy. Trust doesn't come easily to her, but she'll have to trust someone if she wants to put everything to right for good.

Backstory

Who?

Where is she emotionally, mentally, physically the day BEFORE the story begins?

Example

When Emily taught in Reedsville, she and Thomas developed feelings for each other. When she left to care for her ailing grandfather in Seattle, Thomas proposed to her. She turned him down, insisting her duty was with her grandfather. Thomas, dejected, said nothing to anyone. After her grandfather's recovery, Emily decided to accept Thomas's proposal. She could teach for a year and become endeared to the community. Then she and Thomas would marry, and she could establish a Ladies' Aid Society and other social and charitable groups, the way a woman of proper social standing would. Afraid he would return a letter from her, the story begins as she arrives in Portland on her way to Reedsville to accept Thomas's proposal. She's played many roles in the past. She can play this one long enough for it to become true.

- What does she want (the external goal as the story opens)?
- Why (motivation)?
- What keeps her from getting it?
- What's the Dark Moment in her past (write it out as a specific scene)
- What's her deep emotional wound?
- The lie she believes
- The fear she's trying to avoid
- Her emotional response to the Dark Moment that motivates her behavior going forward.
- What was her happiest moment in the past (write this out as a specific scene)?
- How has that lead to her deepest desire (internal goal)?
- What would it cost her to get it?
- What will getting it mean to her?
- What is the emotional opposite of the Dark Moment?
- Her flaw flows from her Dark Moment and is her coping technique to protect her wound that results from the Dark Moment.

Do it

After working on these questions, write three scenes in chronological order from the backstory.

- One is the Dark Moment
- One is her Happiest Moment
- One is a time when she acted on the worldview created by her Dark Moment that reinforces her flawed worldview.

Now write the ending knowing these whys *have to be resolved. See the section on Act III for more help.*

Example

Dark Moment scene: Emily was told when she accepted Jesus into her heart that she would be a new creature. She attended a town social and was completely shunned. All she wanted to do was to be accepted as part of "normal" society, but they didn't believe her.

Happiest moment scene: Emily had a tea party and felt like a true lady.

Reinforcing worldview scene: She will lie to someone about her past, and it will go better for her than if she told the truth.

Act I

The Tipping Point

The story opens on the page when:

- Life can no longer go on the way it has been
- Something threatens her worldview
- We have a sense that all is not what it seems, all is

not well

- A sense that big changes are coming

The Inciting Incident

- Given her past, what event would compel her to react and begin the external goal quest?
- An event ignites her external goal and forces her to face her fear.
- It creates the tension between the desire to keep things the same and to reach for her internal goal.
- It calls into question a long-held belief.

Example

Emily finds money in her bag that she thinks her "grandfather" stole and stuck in her bag before she left. She wants to do the right thing and get the money back to its rightful owner. But she already talked Josh into driving to Reedsville against his better judgment because she was so set on seeing Thomas. Determined not to let Grandfather derail her plans any longer, she decides to go to Reedsville and write to her grandfather to determine who the money belongs to.

Protagonist

Must be:

- Relatable
- Flawed
- Vulnerable
- Able to make the reader care about her
- Wants to get the most by giving up the least, making things worse.
- Must confront the thing she's been avoiding.

External Goal

What she thinks she wants, and what she is striving for.

- Must be able to last a whole novel
- Have stakes that escalate
- Create a real problem for her if it fails
- Creates a ticking clock
- Forces her to make an inner change
- Costs her big emotionally.

Act II

The Inciting Incident and the Ending are two tent poles holding up your story. You know the beginning and the ending. The Backstory and the Why give you the info for Act II.

Act IIA

She tells someone her Dark Moment story from her past. This generates empathy with the reader.

Act IIB

She tells someone her Happiest Moment story and begins to understand why she does what she does, based on her past. Now to make amends.

Obstacles

Come from her internal emotional and psychological barriers.

- What is she scared of?
- Why does she believe she'll fail?
- How does achieving one goal force her to abandon another goal?

- What values would achieving that goal violate/compromise?

Subplots

- Occur often after a major twist, turning point, or revelation.
- Supply info that affects the main storyline
- Make her quest harder
- Deepens our understanding of her

Scenes

- Must have a goal (What does she want?)
- Must have a cause and an effect
- Must matter (What will it cost her?)
- Must have her realize something
- And so? Now what must happen?

Scene Turning Points

- Secrets
- Lies
- Mine the past for people, conflict, misbeliefs

Plot = Action + Reaction + Decision

- Each scene must influence the next one.
- The "why" of each action, reaction, and decision must make sense given her worldview.
- Nothing else belongs on the page.

Story isn't what happens; it's how she reacts to what happens

- Show her train of thought as she reacts to
  everything.
- Show her figuring out how to deal with the latest
  action.
- Show her figuring out how to still achieve her
  goals.
- Show the "why" as she is figuring it out.

Ask "Why?" of everything.

Ask "And so?" of everything.

Write what you know *emotionally.*

Act III

The End We're Driving for from the Beginning

Know your ending before beginning. It must contain these elements to be satisfying.

- A glimpse of her Happily Ever After or happiest
  moment or desire in the first scene must come
  true in some fashion at the end.
- Emotional satisfaction is more important than
  how the plot wraps up.
- The external goal does not have to be achieved.
- She has to face her biggest fear (relive her Dark
  Moment) to experience change.
- Her lie is proved to be a lie.
- Her wound is visibly healed.
- Her deepest desire is reached or reachable.
- Her change must have been earned.
- She must come back to where she started the

story—literally or figuratively—to show how she is different.

The Black Moment

- Ushers in Act III
- Triggered by an Aha! moment of clarity that gives her the courage and strength to engage in "final battle."
- OR the Aha! moment comes after she realizes she feels different than she expected to.
- The lie must feel real in the moment, but she realizes it isn't, based on everything she's learned in Act II.
- Her wound is healed.

Overview

Story Level

ACT I

- Ordinary World
- Inciting Incident
- Great Debate

First chapter must show her to be at least two of these:

- Sympathetic
- Admirable
- Heroic
- Likable
- Funny
- Relatable

Internal Level

ACT I

- Coping with the wound based on the lie generated from the Dark Moment
- Life can no longer go on the same way
- Do I or don't I?

Reveal her:

- Identity (attire, first impressions)
- Purpose
- Skill/superpower/gift
- Reaction to stress
- Insecurity
- Belonging

Deepen all of these throughout the story

Transition

Act I ends and Act II begins when she decides to walk through the door brought about by the Inciting Incident—a point of no return—that begins the adventure.

Story Level

ACT II

- Disappointments
- Difficult decisions
- Competing Values
- Public Stakes

- Private Stakes
- Attempt to solve problem by cheating, but makes it worse
- Disaster
- Destruction

Act IIA

She tells someone the story of her Dark Moment

Act IIB

She tells someone the story of her Happiest Moment

The fight

- Taste of death
- Taste of victory
- Drive toward the Black Moment

Internal Level

ACT II

- Choices reveal values and Backstory
- Goals and values come into conflict
- She does something she would never do given her Worldview and Backstory.
- Sees her greatest desire
- Sees her flaw for what it is

Transition

Act II ends and Act III begins with the Black Moment. Devastation occurs, and all seems to be lost.

Story Level

ACT III

- Black Moment
- Her Dark Moment from the past is resurrecting itself
- Final battle armed with the truth
- Happily Ever After
- All plot threads resolved
- Circle back to the beginning (literally or figuratively) to show change

Internal Level

ACT III

- The lie feels real
- All she has learned refutes the lie
- Aha! moment
- Wound is healed
- She is changed by the truth
- Her greatest dreams (symbolized by her Happiest Moment in the past) are realized.

For a deeper dive on the Novel Blueprint, check out TandemServicesInk.com for books, classes, and a membership site. Get *Posts from the Pencildancer: Short Bites to Improve Your Writing Today* just for signing up for our updates here: https://pages.convertkit.com/b135e30d1c/d6c1fe6895

Chapter 1
LAYING THE FOUNDATION

It's all about emotions

THE BEST BOOKS are created when we the reader identify emotionally with the hero and take the emotional roller coaster ride with him. It's all about emotions. And those are best created by compelling characters.

Think about some of your favorite books. What's the first thing you think of? The message? The theme? No, you remember how it made you feel and the characters. Maybe even the journey they went on.

So let's learn how to create this kind of story. But first, let's dig a bit deeper and discover why this kind of story works.

Brain science and storytelling

It all goes back to how our brains are wired for story. The brain has two goals: survive and thrive. And it is constantly looking for information on how to do this.

Luckily for us, it is particularly wired to get this information from story. If we think about how we convey important information, it is almost always done through story. Think about Aesop's fables or the parables of Jesus. These give us important information about how to behave in society in a format we can easily remember. Every culture has their own stories about important information.

Because of the brain's obsession with surviving and thriving, it casts itself as the protagonist in the story. It wants to learn about physical survival such as, if I encounter a tiger that wants to eat me, what should I do? If you're reading a book that involves that, the brain will go, "Aha! Now I know what to do in that situation."

But the brain also wants to thrive, to know how to deal with emotional and social situations. Which, let's be honest, are far more fraught with land mines and are situations we encounter far more often than tigers anyway.

Romance, women's fiction, and genres that you wouldn't think of as action packed give the brain information on how to navigate and survive the arenas of the heart and social situations. Knowing how to navigate a community, be a part of it, and resolve conflict are extremely important to surviving and thriving.

Stories have a structure the brain is intrinsically looking for. Which makes storytellers some of the most powerful people in the world. The brain needs to know the main character so it can identify with her. And it's looking for information in a certain pattern. Such as this one.

The main character has a past with a wound and a lie that stems from that wound. She has been living life just fine, thank you very much, protecting her wound.

Until something happens. This is the inciting incident, the event that changes everything and means she can no longer operate in the world the way she has been. She wants something external and tangible, a story goal, but what she really wants, deep down inside is the magic elixir that will heal her wound. This is her internal goal.

Because we are resistant to change, she will try to reach for her story goal while protecting her wound. But we as authors will throw all sorts of things at her to make life more difficult, such as conflict and plot complications, because we all know life isn't easy. And the brain knows it too. It doesn't give credit to an easy victory. These will force her to deal with her wound, but generally she'll just make things worse for herself.

Until she reaches the point where her wound is exposed, the lie seems real, and all appears to be lost. The black moment. It is here that she realizes what she needs to do to find healing. She has become stronger and learned more during all her trials.

This leads to the epiphany. The lie is exposed for what it is. She does the thing she needs to do, which she can now do that she couldn't at the beginning of the story. She may need to fight a final battle with the new-found strength and courage, or she might be able to directly tie up loose plot threads. All of which leads to a satisfying conclusion.

Brain science in action

Got it? It sounds familiar, doesn't it? Let's show how this works in an example. I like to use *Star Wars*, the original one, because either most people have seen it or they are familiar enough with the characters and the concepts to get the idea.

Luke Skywalker, our main character, has a past that includes parents who died under unknown (to him) circumstances. His wound is that he longs for adventure, for something more, but he's never going to get it living under the shadow of his father's death. The lie he believes is that he'll never do great things, he's not capable, he's not enough.

He's living with his aunt and uncle on a farm until one day a droid shows up with a holographic message from Princess Leia. He has a choice. He can ignore the message and go on with his life. Or he can accept this invitation to adventure by tracking down old Ben Kenobi and figure out what the message means. This is the inciting incident.

The story goal is to rescue Princess Leia. That's what starts us on this journey. But what he really wants—what will heal his wound—is to fight for the rebellion and be part of something bigger than himself.

We have a lot of plot complications from the asteroids to being captured by the Empire to the death of Obi Wan to the space battle.

Which brings us to the Dark Moment. The Rebels are trying to bomb the Death Star, but nothing is working, and soon it will be in position to blow up the Rebel base. Luke fears he is good for nothing and can't help those he loves.

His epiphany? Obi Wan appearing to him and telling him to use the Force. He's able to drop the bombs precisely and save the day.

Key story points

- Everything in the story must be there for a reason. The brain is looking for answers so it's going to assume if it's in the story, it must be part of the answer.
- Everything must tie itself to the wound in some way. The wound is the problem that the brain is looking for a solution to. Anything else isn't relevant.
- Everything must resolve itself in a reasonable way.

The brain wants the story to make sense so it can be replicated.

After all that, it should be obvious that the main score-card we are going to use to determine if our writing is successful is emotion. We are looking to create an emotionally compelling experience for the reader. You've heard write what you know? I follow Lisa Cron's take on this which is, Write what you know "emotionally."

In everything we do in writing, we are using emotions as the scorecard to judge whether or not we are successful. Even if something is technically correct, if it doesn't engage the emotions, it's not working.

Apply it!

- Pick three of your favorite books in the genre you are writing.
- Why are they your favorites?
- How did they make you feel?
- What made them so compelling?
- What can you take away to apply to your own writing (you might not be able to answer this but it's worth pondering)?
- What emotion do readers in your genre expect to feel?

Chapter 2

THE BIG PICTURE OVERVIEW

Which comes first: character or plot?

AS A WRITER you might find this question paralyzing. Or freeing. The answer is: There is no right answer. Every story will be different. Sometimes you'll have a great idea for a character but won't know what to do with her. Other times the plot will come to you first and you'll have more of a challenge creating a character. Sometimes you'll ping pong back and forth between the two. And as you'll see, having a plot that plays to your character's strengths, fears, and the lies she tells herself will create that compelling emotional experience that readers are longing for. Therefore you will be creating both characters and plot in tandem to some extent.

So let's start with what I call the nugget. That kernel of an idea you have for your story. And let's see what we can make it blossom into.

The what if?

We usually have a nugget of an idea for a story, something that intrigues us that we want to explore more fully through our novel. Which means there are some questions we're going to ask ourselves to begin to flesh out our story.

Whose story is it?

Who is our main character? We don't need to know too much at this point. We will be drilling down into them more and more, but begin to make note of what you do know and some ideas you might want to explore

What's happening?

Again, you might not have a lot of details, but begin to think about the story and jot down some ideas as they come to you.

Hint at the lie

Since the lie is going to be so central to our story, it's never too early to begin thinking about what that might be for your character. Different kinds of lies will drive different kinds of stories.

What's the theme?

Often this isn't something you know right away. It can often develop as you write the story. But theme can help you focus on character issues, plot, and tone. So if you know it or have a general idea of what it might be, make a note of that. A book with a theme of forgiveness would look very different than a book with a theme of justice or vengeance. What parts of the characters you bring out and what plot points you include will be influenced by theme.

Do you remember in English class having an essay question on what the theme of a particular novel was? Or perhaps it was worded as, "Why did the writer write this book?" (To which one of my smart-aleck classmates replied, "To make money." Clearly he didn't know the publishing world.) It sounds so stuffy and intellectual, but it's really not complicated.

Theme is the "why" of your story. It's the "lesson learned." I put that in quotes because I want you to use that term lightly. No one likes a preachy story. But, by the time your character has completed her journey, you, your reader, and even your character should be able to say what she has learned about life from her adventures through this book. If you can do this, then it means your story makes sense.

We all want to understand, at some level, why things happen to us. We want to know they happen for a reason (even if we may not understand that for many, many years). You may know this when you begin writing your story. You may not know it until you finish writing your story. Either way is fine. In fact, sometimes it's worse if you know it at the beginning because you might begin to write to an agenda. And that does not make for good fiction.

When you have real characters based on all the work you did on their backstory and how well you've gotten to know them while you were writing their story, the theme will most likely come naturally from the lie they believe and the truth that sets them free somewhere during the dark moment. It's this epiphany that allows them to overcome the dark moment that plays directly into the theme.

What are the themes of *Star Wars*? There can be more than one.

- Community is better than being a loner (Han Solo).
- Your dreams can come true even if they seem impossible (Luke Skywalker).
- Even when all seems lost, there is hope in the next generation (Obi Wan).

In *Coming Home*, Becca finds true love and acceptance within community. She finds a greater sense of herself there than in the big world of the university.

Okay, now that we have our nugget, let's take a high-level view of plot. It's important to know what all the pieces are that we will need, so let's discuss those before we begin to apply them to our story.

Remember, there are three parts of a plot, layers if you will, that you must keep in mind and juggle together:

- The big picture: three act structure, Hero's Journey
- The medium picture: Action scenes and reaction scenes
- The small picture: stimulus-response sequences

Big picture

A basic three-act structure is a good way to begin. It feels most familiar to us because most movies are done this way.

- The beginning is the first 25% of the book, ending usually where the hero makes a decision or walks through a door where there is no going back
- The middle is the next 50%, where the bulk of the story takes place and usually closes out with the moment where the stage is set for the "final battle" and everything looks pretty bleak.
- The end is the last 25%, where the hero is tested, her true values reveal themselves, she achieves her goal, and plot threads are tied up.

There's also the Three-Disaster Structure, which similarly corresponds. Each disaster creates a transition point. The first disaster is the end of Act I. The second disaster is in the middle of Act II, and the final disaster ushers in Act III.

Let's look at *Star Wars as an* example to make this more concrete.

Act I ends with storm troopers killing Luke's aunt and uncle which pushes him into joining forces with Obi-wan and the Rebellion. It's a disaster, and it drives Luke to a decision.

Act II has a disaster in the middle of Darth Vader killing Obi-wan, which allows Luke and his cohorts to escape the Death Star and take its plans back to the Rebel stronghold.

Act III begins when the Rebels realize the Death Star has tracked them to their hideout (disaster!) and is now hunting them. This leads to the final battle.

A word about Disasters. That's a piece of terminology that might trip you up. It does not mean that something has to blow up or the world has to come to an end. If you are writing a *Mission Impossible* type story, it actually might. But for most of us, the Disasters might be more emotional. Something embarrassing, humiliating, or devastating. So don't let that word create a problem for you. Think of it as a shorthand for a thing your character really, really doesn't want to have happen.

Here are a few questions to help you uncover this:

- Worst thing that could happen?
- What is the secret they don't want anyone to find out?
- What is the lie they believe?

After our three Disasters comes the Ending. Where are we going to end the story? If we don't know the ending, we don't know where we're headed, so we need to have a general idea from the beginning where we need to end up.

Now, let's take these pieces and combine them with our nugget to create the beginning building blocks for our blueprint.

We will return to this blueprint over and over again, refining it and using it to guide our story, so it's worth spending the time here.

The Snowflake Method

You may have heard of the Snowflake Method (http://www. advancedfictionwriting.com/articles/snowflake-method/). If you use Scrivener (and I highly recommend Scrivener—see Resources section), there is a template included there. I like this method for two reasons. One, it helps breakdown the whole process of writing to that of eating an elephant: one bite at a time. Two, it quickly lets you try out different story ideas to see how far you can take them with just a few hours' investment instead of weeks or months of writing.

Now this is a plotting method, so we're only going to use the first two steps here. And it's a good example of making a tool your own. It's good to try different tools and takeaway from them what you find useful and discard the rest. Ready? Let's begin.

One-paragraph summary

We're going to create a one-paragraph summary of our story that we have so far. This isn't set in stone, and it likely will change as your story develops more, but it's a good starting point. Additionally, this is something you will use as the basis for your back cover copy and your ad copy, so you'll get a good return on your time investment.

The biggest problem most people have with these is they try to cram too much in. Look at the *Star Wars* example. We know it's a lot more than just Luke joining the rebellion. But we don't need all of that in there. We just need to grab the reader's attention.

Start with one sentence to set the story up

Who is our character, and what's going on? Don't worry about getting it perfect.

- Don't use character names. Your readers don't know (or care) who your characters are yet. Instead, give us a description that characterizes them. A great way to do this is to use a noun (their skill, a trait, or their competency) plus an adjective (their emotional state).
- Tie together big picture and personal picture. What's at stake? What do they have to lose?

Examples

Star Wars. A disillusioned farmer joins the Rebellion against the star-system gobbling Galactic Empire.

From my book, *Coming Home*. A strong-willed young woman must discover her brother's killer before she's the next victim.

One sentence for each of the three main disasters in the story

Now, we're going to expand into a full paragraph by fleshing out the plot. Using the three-act method, we'll have a disaster/turning point between Act I and II, another in the middle of Act II, and the final one between Act II and III, which often is also the Black Moment.

Throughout this paragraph summary, weave in theme, the internal issues—which we'll talk more in-depth about—and the external plot goal.

Examples

From *Star Wars*.

A young farmer dreams of adventure but lives in a galaxy torn by war. After his aunt and uncle are killed by the Empire for the droids he possesses—one of which has a mysterious message from a princess—he follows his mentor's urging to join the battle. They join a smuggler for cheap transportation in an attempt to rescue the princess. This results in their capture by the Empire. While they succeed in rescuing the princess, in the struggle to escape, the mentor sacrifices himself. After the farmer, the smuggler, and the princess escape, they learn the Empire has followed them to the Rebel base, intending to destroy the planet. In an attempt to exploit the weakness of the Empire's destructive weapon and save the Rebellion and his new friends, the farmer must overcome his natural limitations and draw on the lessons of his mentor.

From my romantic suspense, *Flash Point*.

A directionally-challenged architect stumbles unknowingly onto a crime scene when the contractor who gave her directions turns up missing. In her attempt to help the police with the search, she becomes a target, and her house is broken into and vandalized. One of her in-progress buildings is burned down, and she begins to lose clients. And when she goes to check out another project, she falls through a sabotaged floor into the basement and breaks her ankle. In the end, she has to trust those around her and face her fear of fire by rescuing the man she loves.

Because this is a romance, I would also create the same snapshot from the hero's POV. And then when I write the back cover copy, I'll blend the two together. Here's his version.

A performance-driven firefighter has had his eye on Sarah for a while, but his life as a firefighter keeps getting in the way of romance. By the time he has a chance to ask her out, someone else has beaten him to it. But he has problems of his own. One of the men under his command has a drug problem. The woman who nearly ruined his friendship with his best friend is running a fund-raising campaign for the fire department and he is ordered to cooperate with her. And his nosing into the arson investigation on Sarah's project gets him in trouble with the brass at work, potentially costing him his next promotion. In the end, he has to be honest with Sarah about his past and realize he doesn't always have to be the rescuer.

From *Coming Home.*

A strong-willed woman comes home to 1881 Oregon to bury her brother, her only relative, killed in a logging accident. When rumors of ghosts, accidents at the logging camp, and overheard conversations convince her that her brother's death wasn't an accident, instead of returning to college, she's determined to prove it and get justice. On a walk in the woods she is attacked but manages to escape before serious harm. Then her house is burned down; it's clear someone wants her to leave. After a goldmine is discovered under the logging camp, the secret is out and the mastermind behind the plan sets the camp on fire, which heads toward town and threatens everyone's lives and livelihoods.

If you are writing a series or a big novel with several main characters, you'll want to do this for all of them so you'll have a good sense of who they are and where they need to go in the story. This doesn't have to be set in stone. It likely will change as you dig deeper into you characters—next chapter —but it will give you a general idea of the direction to head. Or let you know if you need to change things up completely. It's much easier to change a paragraph than a whole novel.

Okay, we've swiped a broad brush across the page and have a high-level view of what our story might be about and who might be populating it. In the next chapter, we are going to dig deeper into creating our characters, ones that will engage our readers emotionally.

Apply it!

- Do the first two steps of the Snowflake method for your book. Don't worry if they aren't perfect or even right. The point is to begin the process and start getting stuff on paper. It will change. I guarantee it!
- For each of the main characters, identify:
- Worst thing that could happen?
- What is the secret they don't want anyone to find out?
- What is the lie they believe?

Chapter 3

BACKSTORY

A GOOD BOOK has a compelling character who does something worth watching. Readers will follow a great character through a bad plot, but they won't follow a poorly rendered character through a great plot. And this confirms what we know from brain science. The brain wants to identify with the protagonist, so we have to make the protagonist worth identifying with.

Most writers will find that they are better at either plot or character creation. Or, it may change, depending on the project. With these steps you should be able to do both well.

Characters need:

- A backstory (often where sympathy, fear, and motivation come from)
- A goal
- A worldview

Backstory

Backstory is everything that has happened to your character up until the moment the book starts. The reader doesn't need to know most of it, but you do. When you know your character's backstory, you'll know key things that will influence your plot.

Such as:

- The lie she believes
- Her biggest fear
- Her biggest secret
- What dark moment wound from her past created her current worldview.
- Her happiest moment that she wants to re-create.

Backstory is just like research. You gather a ton of information that you may not actually use. But there are two important things to remember about backstory. One, you need to drip it out in small amounts. Sprinkle it in like breadcrumbs only when it's absolutely necessary. Not even the hero is aware of how much his past is influencing his current actions. And the reader is meeting your hero and getting to know him. The biggest mistake beginning writers make is telling their readers all about how the hero got to where she is today. Do not do that. Nobody cares. Yet.

Think of it this way. When you meet someone at a party, do you immediately tell them your whole life story? No. They would look at you like you're crazy and back away as fast as they can. Your readers will do the same thing if you dump your character's history on the page in the first two chapters. Let it come out over time naturally, the same way you do in real life. You slowly let people in on who you are and where you've been as you get to know them.

Two, the backstory absolutely influences this story. Your character, like all of us, is a result of her life up to this point. In fact, a wound from her past has led her up to this moment when the story begins. Because of this wound, she has been living life a certain way, based on a lie or a misbelief.

But the inciting incident threatens that world view and now everything is going to change. The whole story is her battling against that change and the events of the story forcing her to change so that by the final battle, she no longer believes the lie and is able to be victorious and changed.

See how you can't separate plot from character?

Examples of how backstory is revealed:

- In *Star Wars,* we don't know how Obi-Wan knows Darth Vader or Luke's father until well into the second act when they are on the Millennium Falcon and Obi-Wan is training Luke.
- In *Hunt for Red October,* we don't know why the Soviet captain is defecting until the action is well under way.
- In *Coming Home,* we don't know why Becca was so afraid to return home until well into the second act, though there are small hints that she and Seth have a connection.

The day BEFORE your story begins

Let's take a short step back and think about your character the day before the story begins. Now, you might not quite know where the story will open. We'll get to defining that more precisely in a later chapter. But by now you have enough information to have a general idea of where your story begins.

- Where is she emotionally, mentally, physically the day BEFORE the story begins?
- How is she coping with her back story?

We need to know this so we get an idea of what her wound is, how she is protecting it, and how we can rock her world with an inciting incident.

In *Flash Point*, architect Sarah feels like her life is calm and steady, just the way she likes it. Her best friend is now safe from a terrible incident and a potential love interest is on the horizon. Things are good at work and everything is okay. Because she hates conflict and values peace and calmness, she thinks all is well in her world. She doesn't mind that she never talks to her parents because she has good friends and a fulfilling job.

The Why

Answering these questions helps you build characters with depth and dimension. It will also give you specific ideas of things that must happen in the story as a result of your character's past. You'll spend the most time here out of any part of the Novel Blueprint. And that's because these are the crucial building blocks to the foundation of your story.

The first three questions you can handle at a surface level right now. We'll go more in-depth later. But come up with some basic answers that we can begin to work with, and we'll refine as we go along.

- What does she want (the external goal as the
  story opens)?

This is the simple, obvious story goal. *She wants a promotion.* This can, and often does, change throughout the story. The hero may not even get this goal in the end, but you can still have an emotionally satisfying ending if she gets what she really wants—her internal goal. More on this later.

- Why does she want this particular goal
  (motivation)?

This will vary based on your character. Does she want the prestige, the pay raise, to get away from her cubicle-mate? Maybe she needs a raise to afford her mother's medicine.

- What keeps her from getting it?

A person from another department is better qualified, her boss hates her, she blew her last presentation. These are the obstacles and conflicts that will pepper your storyline. We'll talk more about conflict in the next chapter, but remember that the harder your hero has to fight for what she wants, the sweeter the victory and the more emotionally engaged the reader will be.

- What's the Dark Moment in her past (write it out
  as a specific scene).

It's important that this is written out as a scene. It needs to feel active and alive. This is the event that created the wound in your character's life. There might have been a series of events, but we are distilling them down into one poignant scene. Your hero will tell it to someone in Act IIA, making us even more emotionally involved with him.

For example, in *Flash Point*, Sarah's house burned down when she was little, killing her little brother and sending her mom into clinical depression. She relives this story for Joe as if she was there again, making for an emotionally powerful scene.

- What's her deep emotional wound?

This is where we really get to the good stuff. What's the wound that results from the Dark Moment scene? What's the thing she never wants to go through or feel or experience again? Think of Scarlett O'Hara in *Gone with the Wind* "I swear I will never go hungry again!" This is the thing she goes to great lengths to avoid experiencing. And of course, you will make her experience it in some form during the Black Moment.

- The lie she believes.

This is the rationalization that comes from the Dark Moment and the Wound. It's what she tells herself to cope and to move forward. *I'm not smart enough or brave enough. I don't deserve love like that. I'll never be successful.* It may not be a fully conscious thought but it's there informing her actions, what she does and does not do. When you get to the Black Moment of your story, the lie will feel real. But at the Epiphany it will be proved to be a lie.

- The fear she's trying to avoid.

This also stems from everything we've just dug up. If she doesn't believe she's smart enough or brave enough, she's going to avoid situations where she has to be smart or brave. She's afraid she'll fail.

- Her emotional response to the Dark Moment that motivates her behavior going forward.

This will vary based on your character's personality, which we'll talk about next. If she's a strong-willed type, she might run headlong into conflict or scary situations. Scarlett O'Hara rebuilt her plantation so she'd never go hungry again, running the farm equipment herself. Other types might avoid conflict or always try to be helpful or make people laugh as a coping mechanism. Whatever they do, it's to keep people far away from their wound. And it's been working. Up until the inciting incident.

- What was her happiest moment in the past (write this out as a specific scene)?

Just as we need to know what makes our hero wounded, we also need to know what is the one thing she really, truly wants but never believes she'll get. Like with the Dark Moment scene, we want to write this out as a scene so we can feel the true emotional impact of it. Then we want to hint at it at the beginning of the story. Yes, she has the external story goal, but re-creating this happiest moment is her true internal goal, her heart's deepest desire.

And like with the Dark Moment story, she'll share her Happiest Moment story with someone, usually in Act IIB (another way to prevent a saggy middle). And as you know by now, at the end she'll need to see this come true in some form.

In *Flash Point*, Sarah's happiest moment was being part of a friend's large family who took her camping and made her feel loved and welcomed and not alone. That's re-created at the end of the book with her new friend group.

- What would it cost her to get it?

For anything to have value, it must cost us something. And it's true with the characters too. To get this deepest, internal goal, she's going to have to give up something. And it's going to cost her. In fact, the more precious it is, the more it will cost her.

In *Flash Point*, Sarah is going to have to risk herself and wade into conflict, which she hates. She has to be vulnerable and honest with no guarantee that the outcome will be peaceful.

- What will getting it mean to her?

This is the true satisfaction at the end of the book that makes all the pain, obstacles, and conflict worthwhile. At the beginning of the book, she's living in a world that's okay. She's settling, she's getting by. And she's trying to convince herself that it's enough, living without her deepest desire. Because at the beginning of the book, she's not ready to pursue it. She doesn't think she's capable. A big part of the journey and obstacles are to show her that she is strong enough and to teach her the lessons she needs to learn.

In *Flash Point*, Sarah learns that she needs people; she's not self-sufficient. And to truly be in a relationship, you have to be vulnerable and honest and risk conflict to get what you really want.

Whew! That's been a lot of work! But it's worth it to create characters that leap off the page into your readers' hearts.

Apply it!

- Write your main character's backstory based on what you've discovered.
- What's her deep emotional wound?
- What's the lie she believes?
- What's the fear she's trying to avoid?
- What's her emotional response to the Dark Moment that motivates her behavior going forward?
- What will it cost her to get her internal goal (Happiest Moment relived)?
- What will achieving her internal goal mean to her?

After working on these questions, write three scenes in chronological order from the backstory.

- One is the Dark Moment
- One is her Happiest Moment
- One is a time when she acted on the worldview created by her Dark Moment that reinforces her flawed worldview.

Now begin to sketch out the ending knowing these whys have to be resolved.

$$\rule{6cm}{0.4pt}$$

Chapter 4

CREATING COMPELLING CHARACTERS

WE JUST SPENT a lot of time doing a deep dive on our characters and the ingredients we need to create backstory for them. But that's not enough. They also need to have a personality. Two different personalities would react differently to the same events. And that gives us a lot of room for creativity.

While you are beginning to build your character's backstory and personality, keep these qualities in mind. Your protagonist must:

- Be relatable
- Be flawed
- Be vulnerable
- Be able to make the reader care about her
- Want to get the most by giving up the least, making things worse. Basically, she's cheating, seeing how little she can get away with in regard to changing or confronting her issues. And it usually just makes things worse.

- Confront the thing she's been avoiding. At some point, she has to deal with the wound and the lie. She doesn't want to, but she must in order to get her Happiest Moment.

While we've been covering this information, you've likely known some of the answers to the questions you need to know about your characters. And some you don't know. There are a lot of different resources to use in fleshing out your characters. Some you might like, some you might not. Over time, you'll find the best way for you to get to know your characters.

You need to write down what you learn about your characters so you have some consistency, and you can refer to it while you're writing. It's amazing how much you think you'll remember that you actually forget. So write it down! Scrivener is great for this.

Personality types

I always start here. Then you can move to the information below to flesh her out even more. But personality type gives you information on how your characters like to function in the world, how they make decisions, what kind of structure they like, all of which will tell you what you need to do to make them uncomfortable.

You can use Myers-Briggs, DISC, 5 Voices, or any other personality system that you like. But by far, my favorite is the enneagram. Because the enneagram is based on wounding and coping with that wound. It's also dynamic and shows how numbers react when stressed or when moving toward health. All things that are wonderful when figuring out how to throw conflict at your character. Ian Morgan Cron's book

The Road Back to You is a great primer on the enneagram. You can also check out the Enneagram Institute's website. See the Resources section for more information.

Character charts

A good way to get to know your characters is to use character charts. There are a ton of them out there (just Google it) and part of the process is figuring out what you need to know about your character for yourself. Not everything on charts are relevant or helpful. I've included a generic one in the Resources section.

Character boards

For the more visual person, a board (literal or virtual) of your characters' rooms, clothes, furniture, or anything about their world that helps you step into it. Pictures of your characters can help you visualize them.

Character interviews

Interview your character about the things we've covered. Keep asking why.

Different styles of interviews can elicit different kinds of information. Is it an interrogation? Therapy session? Job interview? Coffee with a friend? Note body language, nervous habits, and speech patterns of your characters.

Have one character interview another. The information they relay is likely to be different depending on who is doing the interviewing.

Character diaries

If your character kept a diary or a journal, what would be in it? Give her some journal prompts that relate to the above information you are trying to dig up. How does she respond? Ask "what if" questions?

What does their normal day look like?

Character biographies

Write a biography of your character. Talk about important years, events, hobbies, family.

A twist on this is to write an obituary. What was their family background? Who did they leave behind? What did they accomplish? What were they known for?

Other things to consider

Juxtaposition. Put opposite traits and people in your hero's life. This puts the hero in contrast with herself and her surroundings. It acts as a foil, a mirror. It creates tension and conflict. Every character has a problem, even secondary characters. Emotional, spiritual, financial, geographic, personal, and so on. Every area of life is fair game for creating opposites.

Give your character a super power. We talked about giving them a skill, but give them something that makes your character unique. What can she do that no one else can in the story? How does it help bring her back from the black moment? Don't overdo it. It can be fun and humorous. She's a walking jukebox or takes things apart when nervous. Maybe she's mentally or physically strong, a prayer warrior, or Radar O'Reilly from MASH. Weave it into their journey to help them in the black moment.

Interesting note

Many writers are interested in psychology. If you think about it, it makes sense. A huge part of our writing is to figure out what makes people tick. And that's what psychology is about. If you notice, many internal goals will be about belonging or being good enough. These are key questions each person must figure out for themselves.

John Eldredge in *Wild at Heart* says the key life question for men is: Am I good enough? Am I capable? Do I have what it takes? In the book he wrote with his wife, Stasi, *Captivating*, they say the key life question for women is: Am I beautiful? Am I desirable?

Another great resource on this subject is Margie Lawson's classes (more information in the Resources section). She shows you how to bring psychological elements to your writing to make it ring true.

Return to the Snowflake: Character summary

In chapter two, we started with the first two steps of the Snowflake, focusing mainly on plot in our one-sentence and one-paragraph summaries. But now we are going to add the characters in. Whereas steps one and two of the Snowflake are primarily about plot, we need to repeat those steps for the personal story of each main (or even minor) character. Especially include your villain.

Include:

- Character's name
- Summary of their own story line in the book
- Their internal motivation (abstract) tied in with

glimpse of hope (or what the Happiest Moment story represents)
- Their external story goal (concrete)
- Their conflict
- Their epiphany (what is the lie they believe and how it is revealed to be a lie)
- Now create a one-paragraph summary of this character's storyline.

Example from *Coming Home.*

Becca Wilson: Returns to her hometown for her brother's funeral, discovers his death wasn't an accident, and tries to solve the murder without getting killed herself.

Motivation: Justice for her brother. To fulfill a lifelong dream of being loved by Seth Blake.

Goal: To solve the crime, not get killed, win Seth's heart.

Conflict: McCormick and societal convention keep her from solving the crime. Seth's guilt and view of her as a kid keep her from getting his heart.

What does she have to lose? She could lose her life, Seth could break her heart (by not loving her back, by still treating her as a little girl, or by being the killer).

Epiphany: The fire reveals McCormick as the killer, she saves herself and boarding house, she absolves Seth of guilt, she learns to trust Seth and God. She doesn't have to prove she's independent to everyone, and she does need people/Seth/God.

One-paragraph summary: Becca returns from her woman's college to her hometown for her brother's funeral. At first, her girlhood crush, Seth Blake, thinks she should go back to school. She despairs of his ever seeing her as a woman and decides to leave. An overheard conversation and a paper in her brother's belongings make her think his death wasn't an accident. She decides to stay and is attacked in the woods. This convinces Seth to help her and gives Becca a glimmer of hope that they might have a future together. When she goes to the logging camp to investigate, Owen shows her the cut chain and now she knows his death wasn't an accident. The killer burns down the homestead Thomas was building for her, her only physical link to him (she feels guilty because she never came home when he wanted her to). She and Seth head to Portland to get dirt on McCormick and find he has a gold claim next door to the logging camp. Determined to get proof on McCormick, Becca goes over the day again with Owen and finds out Seth usually checks the chains. She feels sick and betrayed. McCormick sets fire to the logging camp. The men are called from church service before Becca can talk to Seth. She helps Maggie save the boarding house. She knows she loves Seth and wants to forgive him. When he asks for forgiveness, she gives it and accepts his proposal to build their life together.

The one-paragraph character summary along with your one-paragraph plot summary begins to look a lot like a synopsis. If you are going the traditional publishing route, you will want to include a character summary in your proposal. It helps the acquisitions editor determine if you've created a character that readers will connect with. Which is also helpful in indie publishing as well, since readers are the same no matter who publishes your book.

Since I originally sent *Coming Home* through the traditional route, here's the polished version I used in the proposal.

Becca Wilson: A strong-willed young woman whose stubbornness is often a cover for her fear and insecurity. After losing her parents and then her brother, she feels she can only trust herself. When she suspects her brother's death isn't an accident, she's forced to accept Seth's help to find justice for her brother. While she's trying to find her brother's killer, he's looking for her too. Because of the threat to her safety, she can't be as independent as she likes. Yet being in such close proximity to the man who's always held her heart threatens her independence with the possibility that her girlhood dream of Seth's love just might come true.

One-page synopsis

Grab the one-paragraph summary from chapter two. We're ready to expand it with all the information we've learned about our characters. Here's an easy way to structure it.

- First paragraph: one-paragraph summary of the story
- Second paragraph: one-paragraph summary of your heroine.
- Third paragraph: If you're writing romance, this paragraph would be about the hero. This is also a good place to put in the villain's paragraph if he is a strong enough presence in the book or any other significant character.
- Fourth paragraph: first disaster
- Fifth paragraph: second disaster
- Sixth paragraph: third disaster
- Seventh paragraph: Black Moment
- Eighth paragraph: wrap it up.

Give the ending away! You won't do that on your actual back copy for your book, but if you are showing this to an editor, you have to prove that you can tie this book up. And you need to know the end that you are aiming for.

How to do this for a series

If you are writing a series, it's a great idea to do these steps for each book in the series before you write the first book. The reason being you need to know if your series idea is strong enough to last at least through the first several books.

If you are writing a series that is centered around a location or a group of people but the hero of each book is different (my Hometown Heroes series is like this), then this is helpful to make sure you have a good grasp on all the characters that could end up being major characters in the series.

If you are writing a series with one major character that has a larger arc that plays out over several books (like the Jack Reacher books), you will also want to do these steps to make sure that each book has a satisfying ending and moves your character farther along on her journey to healing her wound.

Don't forget the villains!

Your villain needs to be a good match for your hero. The harder the hero has to work to overcome the villain, the stronger he becomes. You don't want your villain to be a straw man. Your hero needs a worthy opponent. Readers don't root for a hero that has an easy victory. The brain loves seeing how someone overcomes a difficult challenge. Because, let's face it, we know how to handle the easy stuff. It's the hard stuff we want answers to.

Keys to crafting a good villain:

- Give them as strong motivations for their behavior as your hero has. The more worthy an opponent they are, the better your hero looks for beating him.
- What they are doing needs to seem reasonable to them. Even make them a bit sympathetic.
- Make them believable. The threat has to be real and it is based on what the villain does, not just what he says.
- Make the threat personal to the hero.
- Make it a tangible representation of the hero's biggest fear
- Know your antagonist's motivation. Why is he after the hero? Did she just happen to be in the wrong place at the wrong time? Or is she a specific target? Or does the hero have something the antagonist wants? Or is it a battle of wits, maybe nothing personal, like a cop and a burglar. Either way you need to know what makes him tick and what he wants.

Make sure you can tell the story from the villain's point of view. It's a helpful way to make sure you've crafted a well-rounded villain whose story makes sense to him.

Example from *Flash Point*.

Tony DiMarco is a real estate developer that doesn't mind skirting the law when it suits him. He is motivated by money. If he has enough money he'll be secure, set for life, not doing back-breaking work like his dad did, sending him to an early death. As we dig down, we see he's not really motivated by money, but by security and fear.

His issue with Sarah is not personal, she just has the key piece that keeps him from making a lot of money. First disaster (for Tony), Sarah gets the map from Greg and can place Tony and Greg together (This is Sarah's inciting incident). Second disaster, he orders her home trashed but the map is gone (Sarah's first disaster). Third disaster, he orders her job site sabotaged, but she survives and doesn't seem to be scared off (Sarah's second disaster). In fact, she's putting the pieces together and giving them to the police. His black moment is when he orders his man to bury the evidence on the job site, but his man sets a fire, gets rescued by Sarah, and confesses everything (This is Sarah's final battle).

When you tell the story from the antagonist's POV, it should make sense to him and to us. Remember, they are the hero of their own story, and you should be able to tell the story from their perspective. The emotional tension created by the interaction between the hero and the villain keep readers involved and turning pages.

Apply it!

- Go through the character exercises and personality tests. Don't feel the need to fill them out completely. Some stuff just won't matter for your character. But do give them a read through to see what will be useful. You will be pulling bits and pieces from all of these to make your own chart and exercises. And your characters might surprise you with what they'll tell you.
- Create a character summary for each of your major characters, including the villain.

- Create your one-page synopsis. If you're writing a series, write one for each of your books, or at least the first three.

Chapter 5

GOALS AND MOTIVATION

UP UNTIL NOW, we've mentioned a few times that our characters need goals, motivation, and conflict, but we've only touched on what those mean. Now we are going to do a deep dive into those subjects.

We said in chapter three that characters need three things:

- A backstory (chapter three)
- A goal
- A worldview

We'll talk about the next two in this chapter.

GMC: It's not a car company

Fifteen or twenty years ago, an author (Debra Dixon) wrote a book called *GMC: Goal, Motivation, and Conflict*, and ever since GMC has been used as a writing shorthand term. So it's important that we know what those pieces are. They are key elements for any story.

Goals

As you're developing your character's backstory, you're naturally going to touch on her goals. A goal is simply something your character wants. And to get it, she has to solve a problem (conflict or obstacle). We the readers need to know what this goal is pretty close to the beginning of the story. I have an editor friend that says it needs to be within the first three pages. That's about right.

Until you have a goal, you do not have a story. Goals need to be:

- Clear and compelling. Specific and concrete. The reader should be able to say what it is.
- Established early on. They drive the story forward.
- Important and urgent. Even better if there's a deadline. If not, there's no pressure to complete them.
- Changeable. They can (and should) change throughout the story. Often your character thinks he wants one thing, but as he goes on his journey he discovers he really wants something else (more valuable and deeper) because he has grown and changed.
- Naturally derived from motivations, which we'll talk about next, but which are ultimately rooted in the backstory.
- Costly. Failure to meet the goal should cost the hero something. A goal with a cost for success is even better. This does not mean a financial cost, although it could. But often there's an emotional or relational cost.

The more desperately a character wants something, the more interesting and emotionally involving the plot becomes. So the goal is very much tied to the beginning of the story. You can't have a story without a goal, and you can't have a goal unless you know your character's backstory. See how plot and character are always intertwining?

Now, there are two levels of goals. There are story-level (plot) goals. And each scene also needs a goal, which we will talk about in more detail when we get to scene structure. For now, know that the rules are similar, they just vary in scope. So a story-level goal will be much bigger in scope than a scene-level goal. But they both must have the same characteristics.

A story-level goal might be that your hero wants a job promotion. That's a big enough goal to carry a story. A scene-level goal might be that she wants a cup of coffee. That's not big enough to carry a whole story. But both are specific and clear. Both can be made important, urgent, and costly, just at different scales.

SMART-E goals

Your characters' goals have the same characteristics as the goals for your real life. They are generally SMART-E.

S-Specific. Something concrete, not a vague wish. "I want to go to Chicago."

M-Measurable. We can tell when it's happened. "I want to go to Chicago tomorrow."

A-Actionable. Something you have the ability to achieve. You may want to go to Chicago, but if you are broke or don't have a car, you don't have the ability to get there. It is just a wish.

R-Realistic. You may want to go to Chicago tomorrow,

but if there is a snowstorm, it's not realistic to think you can get there.

T-Time-sensitive. It needs to be done by a certain date. "Tomorrow" is a specific time. In fiction, this can act as a ticking bomb, increasing tension and thus, emotional engagement.

E-Emotionally important. If your character doesn't care about Chicago, given her values in this story, then we won't either. Tie the goal to something she cares about and expresses her values. "I want to go to Chicago tomorrow for my aunt's birthday who's dying of cancer."

Examples

> From *Star Wars*. Luke and Han have rescued Princess Leia, but they are still on the Death Star. Their Goal is to return to Han's ship and escape.
>
> From *Coming Home*. Becca wants to get through her brother's funeral without having an embarrassing conversation with his best friend, Seth.

Two parts: external and internal goals

Goals have two parts to them. An outward story goal that is tangible. And an internal goal to satisfy a longing they may not even be fully aware of.

External goals are:

- Outward and tangible
- What your hero wants and thinks she is striving for

- Must be able to last a whole novel
- Have stakes that escalate
- Create a real problem for her if it fails
- Creates a ticking clock
- Forces her to make an inner change
- Costs her big emotionally

External goal examples

Star Wars: Winning a battle against the Empire.

Coming Home: Finding her brother's killer and bringing him to justice.

Flash Point: keeping her mentor's architectural firm afloat.

Internal goals

But we don't just have an outward, action story arc. Our characters need to grow internally throughout their journeys. So they have an internal goal too. And it might not even be one they're aware of. This is where the backstory that we dug up will begin to morph into motivation. This is where the Dark Moment story, the Happiest Moment story, and the resulting wounds and lies come into play

- It's what she really wants based on her deepest desire/happiest moment/glimpse of hope
- What will it cost her to get it?
- What will getting it mean to her?
- What is the emotional opposite of the Dark Moment?
- Must be resolved in the ending.

Internal goal examples

Star Wars: Luke's inward goal is to be a hero, to bring back honor to his family, and recover from the shame of his father. He wants to belong to something bigger than himself since he's never had much of a family.

Coming Home: Becca wants to belong. She's always had a crush on Seth, but ultimately she wants to create a family and a community with him and those around her.

Flash Point: Joe wants to be accepted for who he is, not the hero he always plays.

This is tied into **the lie your character believes**. Luke believes he'll never leave the farm and amount to anything. Becca believes Seth can never think of her as anything beyond a little girl and that she's not worthy of belonging. Joe believes he's only worth something when he's helping people.

This is also tied into the **glimpse of hope**. This is where we catch a brief glimpse in the beginning of something the hero's heart longs for, but because of the lie she believes, she thinks she'll never get it. Luke gets his dad's lightsaber from Obi-Wan and for a moment, he pictures himself as a Jedi. Becca sees Seth again and meets his eyes, and for a moment, wonders what it would be like to be coming home to him for good. Joe gets a glimpse of a father and son and longs for that kind of unconditional love.

Finally, this is the **lesson she must learn**. Luke learns that even when Obi-Wan is dead, he lives on in Luke's memory, guiding him, so Luke will always belong and be capable. Becca learns that God's plans are best and she cannot try to run away from them, that what is painful is also healing. Joe learns he can let down the mask of performance and still be accepted.

This is the information we have gleaned through developing the hero's backstory.

Your character is ultimately most satisfied by reaching this internal goal. They can fail at their external goal and still have a satisfying ending if they have reached their internal goal.

This leads us nicely into motivation, since that is what makes a goal resonate emotionally.

Motivation

This is the emotional driving force behind why your character wants to achieve her goals. And just like the internal and external goals, there are corresponding internal and external motivations. The worldview flows from all of the backstory we discovered. All of those things combined will affect how your hero sees the world and interacts with it.

Motivations must:

- Follow from values, purpose or noble cause.
- Be the "why" behind the goals.
- Be the kick in the pants to make your character grow and change (because it's uncomfortable and not fun!).
- Bring about conflict. The hero's motivation is so strong that she is desperate enough to not let anything stop her.
- Create a turning point in her life.

As the stakes rise, the motivation has to be strong enough

to overcome them. If your hero doesn't care that much about something, she'll give up pretty easily when things become difficult and the stakes rise. But if making this goal defines the core of who she is, then nothing is going to stop her. And that's what makes readers emotionally engaged and rooting for the characters.

Brandilyn Collins in *Getting Into Character* has the four Ds to get you thinking about your character's motivations and goals and how you can turn them into concrete scenes.

- Distancing—What things will pull your hero away from her dream?
- Denial—The inciting incident or problem at the beginning of the story often makes it seem as if she will never get her dream.
- Destruction—The point on her journey where it seems she's further from her goal than ever.
- Devastation—The black moment where there is no hope and no turning back.
- Delight—Getting her goal and happy ending. An extra one thrown in to make sure we end on a happy note!

James Scott Bell in *Plot and Structure* uses the LOCK system to accomplish the same thing.

- Lead—An ordinary person who develops extraordinary skills throughout the story.
- Objective—Something that is crucial to his happiness or essential to his well being.
- Confrontation—There must be an opposition equally dedicated to stopping the lead.
- Knockout ending—The feeling of satisfaction at the end of the journey.

See how goals and motivations are naturally leading us into a discussion about plot?

Keep asking why

As you are nailing down your character's goals and motivations, keep asking your character why they want their goal until they reveal what noble cause, purpose, or value is met by their desire. What behaviors and traits naturally follow from that inner value?

Now to make it juicier, what's the opposite of that value? We'll expand on this more in the next chapter on conflict, but for now consider how two dearly held values could compete with each other.

Examples of goals with competing values:

Emily wants to return the money in her bag
> Why? Because she wants to do the right thing.
> Why? Because she's a new person.
> Why? Because she's made a spiritual commitment.

Emily wants to keep her past a secret.
> Why? Because she's afraid of what others might think.
> Why? Because she's afraid of rejection again.
> Why? Because she's not that person anymore.

These two values are going to come into conflict, and that's what keeps readers turning pages. Competing values and competing motivations create conflict, which emotionally engages your readers.

Backstory, noble cause, values, and purpose determine motivation which determines goals.

Worldview

After all that, worldview is quite simple. It's the sum of everything that you've discovered about your character and how it all influences how she sees the world and moves through it.

You can give two characters the same goals and obstacles, but if one has a more cheerful personality and has had a less traumatic wound, then they will see the world quite differently than a character who has a more serious disposition and more traumatic wound.

Your challenge as an author is to give each of your characters a unique worldview, one that is different than your own. Have you ever read an author where all the characters seem like the same people with different names? That is what you want to avoid.

Think of the people you are closest to, your friends and family. You all have a slightly different outlook on the world, and that's great. So make sure your characters reflect this reality.

Apply it!

- For your main characters, what are their internal and external goals?
- Look for places where your main characters have desires that compete. How can you sharpen the contrast so that if they get one, they cannot get the other?
- What are the goals and motivations for your villain?

Chapter 6

CONFLICT

WE WILL SPEND a lot of time on conflict because it is one of the hardest areas for writers. We are geared in our personal lives to avoid, minimize, or resolve conflict. It's hard to turn that off and revel in conflict. But that's what we need to do.

This is not just about fighting or arguing. It is better termed **obstacle**, for it's really the series of obstacles that stand in the way of your hero (story-level conflict) or POV character (scene-level conflict) getting her way. You must have this. If your character gets her goal without conflict, that's boring and not emotionally engaging. The value of the goal comes from the struggle. The bigger the goal, the bigger the struggle. What will hinder, block, or complicate her ability to reach her goal?

Just as we talked about story-level and scene-level goals, there is also story-level and scene-level conflict. Conflict will come from what you've discovered about your character and your plot. Your character's goals and motivations should begin to automatically create conflict. As you are learning about your character, you should be thinking of how to create conflict from what you've learned.

Conflict must be believable. We want powerful, original conflicts. But they have to make sense to the reader. There needs to be an underlying logic behind every action your characters take. They need to be motivated by the backstory we have discovered about them. As we have learned about our characters' backstories, we should have a pretty good sense of their inner values and what behaviors and traits naturally follow from that.

But, characters don't always do the smart thing. Everyone has a weakness, a flaw, or something that would cause them to behave irrationally. Maybe an opposing character deceives them into making a mistake, or maybe they deceive themselves and make a wrong move as a result.

Think back to the last chapter when I asked you about your character's competing values. Now, to make it juicier, what's the opposite of that value? What's something your character would never do. What would make her do that? Donald Maass' *Writing the Breakout Novel workbook* has excellent exercises along these lines to use all throughout the story. Because the unexpected also draws readers in emotionally.

Conflict through competing values

- Opposite of what they value
- Something they would never do. What would force them to do it?
- Two competing values that both can't come true

When I first read about having your character do something she'd never do, I thought murder or something equally dramatic. But what we really mean is to dig into that emotional wound. What would make her expose it or what protective method would she never lay down? What value would she never compromise? And when you begin to pit competing values against each other, you develop an emotionally compelling story.

Examples

In *Flash Point,* Sarah is terrified of fire. She'd never personally fight one. And yet she must to save the man she loves.

In *Flash Point,* Joe would never abandon the woman he loves, especially to her greatest fear. But he must to rescue a man in danger of dying.

Sources of conflict

Inherent Conflicts in Plot

- Setting: distance in relationships, bad memories, dangerous environment
- Opponents: different viewpoints, opposing desires and wants
- Relationships: mother and daughter, romantic, siblings, coworkers, and so on

External Conflict

- Outside world pressing in
- Institutions. Banks, the IRS, the FBI, the justice system, schools, work, bureaucracy. Any institution can theoretically be a source of

conflict for a character, given the right situation. It is useful to dramatize the institution through a character who personifies the values and position of the institution. For example, the bank manager who rejects our character's loan.

- Physical Environment. At times the environment itself creates conflict for our character. Roads are slick with snow and ice when she needs to make a fast getaway. The mountain town where she is hiding from a stalker has no cell phone service when she needs to call for help. Years of drought have reduced her cattle herd from hundreds of head to merely dozens.
- Two or more people whose needs or wants are in competition
- People close to the character. Often conflict can arise from those with the deepest emotional ties to your character: family members, a lover, close friends. Problems arising from someone who is so connected to your character will obviously carry heavy emotional burdens. These close connections make conflict emotionally treacherous. Think about who you come into conflict with the most. It's probably your family, close friends, or coworkers—the people that are closest to you. It's because you have a connection that you have conflict. You care about them and their opinions of you and what you do. Or you spend a considerable amount of time in close proximity to them.
- Contributing to the conflict between your main characters may be differences in their personality types. This is why looking at personality types is helpful. However, you cannot carry an entire

book with only different personality types as a source of conflict for your characters. They need a substantial issue to be warring over.

- Individuals in society. Coworkers, a boss, the mother of your child's best friend. Our characters do not have as intense an emotional connection to these people as they do to the ones in the previous category, but these people can still cause serious problems in their lives. For instance, a conflict with her boss could end up with our character losing her job. A conflict with her son's best friend's mother could result in her son being ostracized on the school playground.

However, if you only have external conflict, the plot will feel contrived and manipulated by the author. When creating external conflict, the most successful ones are those that:

- Exacerbate your main character's internal conflict.
- Can be symbolized by a concrete obstacle

Internal Conflict

- Personal issues — doubts, fears, internal turmoil
- Two opposing desires
- Protection against something
- Spiritual struggle
- Major flaw

The richest, most emotionally compelling conflict come

from internal conflict. And of course, you should bake in some inherent conflicts into the plot.

In regard to conflict, we need to:

- Create stories based on premises that are rich in conflict.
- Begin our stories with a dramatic action or event that sets the conflict in motion. We'll talk about this in the next chapter.
- Ensure that at least one of our main characters has an emotional conflict that is preventing her from achieving what she wants/needs in life. If we've done our backstory work right, this will happen.
- Concoct plots that feed the conflict, don't douse it.
- Build conflict in ever-increasing increments.
- Layer conflict for rich, believable stories.
- Seek to be original while striving for believability.
- Resolve the conflict with an emotionally satisfying conclusion. Which is the end we are heading for and why we need to know what it is our characters need to create that ending.

Raising the stakes

It's not enough just to have conflict. Throughout the book, the conflict in each scene should raise the stakes. Something that is important at the beginning of the book might not even matter by the end of the book because the stakes have been raised. This keeps the tension tight and keeps your readers emotionally involved and turning pages. Continually think of how you can make this worse for your character.

There are four main ways to increase the stakes

1. Add more conflict, internal, external, or both. Introduce a new complication to the situation, force a tighter deadline, give the main character a new handicap, or shut-down a potential "exit route." The point is to increase the pressure on your main character. To make her—and the reader—sweat.
2. Make the consequences of failure worse. Put more at risk in your story.
3. Compel the reader to care more. Reveal new facets of your characters to win additional reader sympathy for their plight.
4. Opposites. Put your hero in conflict with herself. Pull her in two opposite but equal directions. How can she want both things simultaneously? What causes that? What steps does she take to pursue those conflicting desires? Readers like characters who have to struggle to earn what they want. Put your hero in impossible situations where no one can win without someone else losing in the process.

Keep in mind that what a character thinks she needs may not be what her innermost self really does need. When it is an unconscious need that is driving your story, you will end up with a complex character and a truly compelling story. Whether your character's internal conflict springs from a state of body, mind, or emotions, your job as writer is to relate all these conflicts to the last one—emotion.

Apply it!

- Identify the sources of conflict contained in your Blueprint. What ideas about conflict spring naturally or potentially simply from the story idea?
- List potential internal conflicts you've uncovered as part of digging into your characters' backstories. What external factors could you add to make these internal conflicts even worse?
- Look for places where your main characters have desires that compete. How can you sharpen the contrast so that if they get one, they cannot get the other?
- Consider the internal and external conflicts you have uncovered in earlier lessons. Jot down five possible ways you could up-the-stakes for each of these conflicts. Can you make any of these ideas work?
- Creating a deadline to increase time pressure
- Saddling one of your main characters with an unexpected difficulty
- Revealing new, unexpected information that will make the situation worse
- For each of your main characters, what's something they wouldn't do under most circumstances? What would force them to do it?

Chapter 7
WHERE EVERYTHING BEGINS

WE HAVE BEEN LEARNING a lot about our characters so we'll know how to put them on the page. In the last chapter, we began to weave in the plot pieces. In this chapter, we'll actually see how all of this begins to come together.

Keep in mind as we talk today that there are not only three acts to a book, there are three layers. These are sort of like the forest and the trees. You must keep them in mind and juggle them together. They are:

- The big picture: three act structure
- The medium picture: Actual scenes
- The small picture: action sequences within scenes

Since we've spent so much time on characters, let's do a quick review of the basic three-act structure before we dig into talking about plot.

The beginning: Act I

- Tipping point
- Inciting incident
- Point of no return
- First disaster

The beginning is the first 25% of the book, ending usually where the hero makes a decision or walks through a door where there is no going back. This is the **inciting incident.** Usually the first disaster falls somewhere around this point and may or may not be the inciting incident.

The middle: Act II

- The bulk of the story takes place.
- Second disaster in the middle
- Reveals his Dark Moment Story
- Reveals his Happiest Moment Story
- The stage is set for the black moment and possibly final battle
- Third disaster.

The middle is where most of the story takes place. There's a second disaster in the middle, the hero reveals his **Dark Moment Story** and his **Happiest Moment Story**. It usually closes out with the moment where the stage is set for the **Black Moment, Epiphany** and possibly **Final Battle** and everything looks pretty bleak, which is the third disaster. The plot and subplots are most fully developed here.

The end: Act III

- Hero is tested
- Her true values reveal themselves
- She achieves her goal (internal and possibly external)
- Plot threads are tied up

Here's where we wrap everything up. Everything that we've been shooting for from the beginning comes to fruition here. The hero is tested and her true values—which she has been learning all along—reveal themselves. She achieves her internal goal and maybe her external one, and plot threads are tied up.

Example: *Star Wars*

- Act I ends with storm troopers killing Luke's aunt and uncle, which pushes him into joining forces with Obi-wan and the Rebellion.
- Act II has the middle disaster of Darth Vader killing Obi-wan, which allows Luke and his cohorts to escape the Death Star and take its plans back to the Rebel base.
- Act III begins when the Rebels realize the Death Star has tracked them to their base and is now hunting them. This leads to the final battle.

So now that we are refreshed on the overview, let's look at the components that make up Act I, where everything begins.

Beginnings

Now that we've created our character and given them goals and problems, let's take a moment to talk about beginnings. How do we introduce our characters to our readers? Where do we begin? Your story needs to **begin the day everything changes**, when your character can no longer continue to live life the way she has been. We start with a little bit of the normal world and then everything changes. Then the hero's goal is to deal with and survive that change and all the other things we throw at her.

Examples

Star Wars. The droids show up at Luke's farm. This is his ordinary world. They say they belong to Obi-Wan, so Luke takes them to Obi-wan and learns about the galactic battle. Obi-Wan asks for his help. He refuses and returns to his farm, only to find it destroyed and his aunt and uncle killed. Life can no longer continue the way it has been, and his goal now is to join the Rebellion and stop the Empire.

Coming Home. We get just a glimpse of Becca's ordinary world as she travels on the stagecoach back toward her old home, to what used to be her ordinary world before going off to college. Her goal at this point is to survive her brother's funeral without having an embarrassing conversation with Seth, the reason she avoided coming home for nearly four years. But everything changes when she realizes her brother's death was not an accident, and her new goal is to find out who killed him and get justice.

Putting it on the page

When we introduce our characters to our readers, it is much like when you meet someone for the first time. You start drawing conclusions about them based on how they dress, carry themselves, how they talk, how they treat other people, and so on. What are they trying to portray to the world around them based on these things?

Like we talked about with backstory, don't give it all in one dump. As we go deeper into the story, we'll get to know deeper levels of the character too. Susan May Warren in *Deep and Wide* shows the process of revealing your characters to your readers based on how far you are in the story. The further you are, the deeper the layers. The beginning of the book is a lot more about surface layers, but as we get into the book, especially toward the Black Moment and Epiphany, we are dealing with deep psychological and heart issues.

All the work you have done on the backstory begins to play itself out in the plot and in gradual increments, not all in one big dump. Now that we have a general idea of how the backstory will flow through the whole plot, let's turn to our beginning, the first chapter.

The all-important first chapter

When we first meet our hero, we need the reader to begin to create an emotional attachment to her. We do that best when we see her in a situation that evokes strong emotion. We have a lot of information on her at this point in our heads and in our charts. So let's use it wisely. That first chapter needs to hook the reader and keep them turning pages.

In the **first scene** we need to see something:

- Sympathetic—She's lost something, or something unfair has happened to her. She's in jeopardy (emotional or physical), a hardship not of her own making, an underdog, vulnerable but not a wimp. We see her determination and inner conflict.
- *Examples:* Becca is on the way to her brother's funeral.
- Luke is looking at the sky, watching a battle that he can't be a part of because he's stuck on the farm.
- Admirable—Show your hero to be highly skilled or ethical. Even a villain can be admirable if they are skilled at what they do.
- In *Flash Point*, Joe is fighting a wildland fire, leading a team, and saving someone's home. He's skilled at what he does.
- Heroic—Save the cat from a tree, rescue a stuck puppy, help an elderly person.
- Joe saves a dog from being crushed by a Phos-check drop.
- Likable—Show her caring about other people, even if it's to her own detriment.
- This is the person who stops to help someone even though we know they're running late for an important presentation.
- Funny—A lot of romantic comedies use this.
- Relatable—Show how she is like us. Not perfect, but with flaws and foibles.
- The girl who spills coffee on herself on the way to an interview or gets splashed with muddy water by a passing car. We've all been there.

So we need to see at least two if not more of those qualities in our hero when we first meet her. The hero needs to be someone the reader wants to follow through the pages of your book. And we know from brain science that the brain wants to learn how to thrive and survive from your book. It can only do that if it sticks with the book. If that emotional attachment is not made early on, the reader will put the book down. We've talked about how important that emotional attachment is and that it is really the only scorecard we are keeping.

By the end of chapter one, we also need to reveal:

- The hero's view of herself
- Her external story goal
- Her internal goal (via the glimpse of hope)
- Her values
- Her skills
- Her reaction to stress
- What makes her feel insecure
- Where she feels she belongs.

Tipping point

Now that we have all of our pieces, let's begin. The story opens on the page when:

- Life can no longer go on the way it has been.
- Something threatens her worldview
- We have a sense that all is not what it seems, all is not well
- A sense that big changes are coming.

Her coping mechanism that has served her so well begins to lose its power. It is **the day everything changes**, when she can no longer continue to live life the way she has been living. Remember when we talked about where your hero was the day *before* the story opens? We need to know that so we have a sense of her state of mind when the story opens. And we rock her world.

Inciting incident

If the tipping point is when the story opens, then the inciting incident is the actual event that rocks her world and forces her to make a change. If her goal before this was to keep everything going the way it had been, then the hero's new goal is to deal with and survive the change.

How to create a compelling inciting incident:

- Given her past, what event would compel her to react and begin the external goal quest?
- An event ignites her external goal and forces her to face her fear.
- It creates the tension between the desire to keep things the same and to reach for her internal goal.
- It calls into question a long-held belief

Example

In *The Road Home*, Emily finds money in her bag that she thinks her grandfather stole and stuck in her bag before she left him [this plays to her fear of having her past discovered]. She wants to do the right thing and get the money back to its rightful owner. But she already talked Josh the stagecoach driver into driving to Reedsville against his better judgment because she was so set on seeing Thomas [opening story goal]. Determined not to let Grandfather derail her plans any longer, she decides to go to Reedsville and write to her grandfather to determine who the money belongs to [new story goal].

It creates tension between her long-held belief that she needs her past to be kept a secret and her desire to be honest and do the right thing.

Star Wars. Original goal, get droids to help with the farm. This is his ordinary world. The droids say they belong to Obi-Wan so Luke takes them to him. Obi-Wan asks for Luke's help. He refuses and returns to his farm, only to find it destroyed and his aunt and uncle killed [inciting incident]. Life can no longer continue the way it has been, and his new story goal now is to join the Rebellion and stop the Empire.

Coming Home. We get just a glimpse of Becca's ordinary world as she travels on the stagecoach back toward her old home, to what used to be her ordinary world before going off to college. Her goal at this point is to survive her brother's funeral without having an embarrassing conversation with Seth, the reason she avoided coming home for nearly four years. But everything changes when she realizes her brother's death was not an accident and her new goal is to find out who killed him and get justice.

Often crafting the first chapter, even the first scene, can take longer than any other part of the book. It's worth spending time on it, even making alternate versions, because it sets the stage for the rest of your book.

Also consider that after you've written the book and learned more about your characters, you may want to come back and revise the beginning once you've written the ending.

Do I or don't I?

At some point, your hero has to make the decision to switch to this new story goal. And that is going to cause some internal debate. Our tendency is toward stasis, toward keeping things the same, so it has to be a compelling reason to make the leap to the new story goal and all that could entail. You want to have a scene or part of a scene where the hero debates with either herself or another person the wisdom of what she's about to do. This will reveal a lot of information about your hero.

Story world

Not only do we introduce our characters in the first chapter, we also reveal the world they live in. We get the first glimpse of the story world, the everyday world of our character. In *Star Wars*, it's a galaxy far, far away. In *Coming Home*, it's 1881 Oregon. It can be as complex as an invented world or as simple as the street blocks between home and school. But a different story world will create a different type of story at every level.

We don't need to spend a lot of time here, but we do want to set the scene and let our readers in on what the ordinary world of our hero is like. There should also be a hint that all is not well, that the waters are stirring underneath the surface. Change is coming.

This is often a good place to reveal the **Glimpse of Hope**. This isn't the full Happiest Moment story. This is just a glimpse of that internal goal, that deep desire that they want but don't actually think they can get. You can think of this often as an image, a house with a white picket fence or a boy playing catch with a dog. They can represent that longing deep inside of your hero. This is ultimately what readers are going to be hoping she gets at the end of the story and the ups and downs of the story will be measured by how close or far she is to getting the longing of her heart. This will be one more way to emotionally attach your reader to your hero.

Consider story world or setting, as it's also called, much like backstory. There is a tendency to set the stage for the reader and give them all the info about the world your hero inhabits. But that works as well as a backstory info dump. It stops the action, and it will make your reader put your book down. Reveal the story world as your characters interact with it. Give us just the information we need in that moment for everything to make sense.

Research

When you are writing a story world that requires a lot of research, there is a tendency to want to put all that hard work to good use. I can't tell you how many hours I've spent tracking down what kind of dress my historical characters would wear for something that's not even a full line in one of my books. But the one bit of line is all the readers care about. Put the rest on your website or Pinterest board so those who are interested can find it and geek out on it.

Most story worlds require some research. Even if you are writing something you know intuitively, you'll still have to do some research to get the details right like clothing, available technology, geography, weather, and a million other details that make a story seem real.

If you are writing a historical novel, you'll likely have to do some research before you can even begin to write your story because some of those facts will directly influence your story. For something you may be more familiar with, you might be able to write your story, mark where you need to answer a question, and move on. I put this in the editing phase. You don't want to stop your creative flow to get bogged down in research.

There are good and bad things to research. The good thing is that, done well, research will skillfully bleed through the pages, giving your reader the illusion that they are in your story. It pulls them into the story world with the hero and enhances the emotional experience.

The bad thing is when a writer wants to put in every bit of research into their story. I get it. Research takes a lot of time and sometimes you uncover really cool facts. But if they don't add to the emotional experience the reader feels then they don't belong. Hint: most of your research won't make it into your book, but it will allow you to write from a place of knowledge and strength.

One other thing about research: If you get something wrong, guaranteed a reader will let you know. And if you keep that thought in the forefront of your brain, it will para-lyze you. So research what you can. Talk to people who know what you want to know. Visit places. And know you still might not get it right. And that's okay.

If you have created your own story world, it's a good idea to keep notes on things, just as if you were researching a real world. You'll want to be consistent throughout your book and your series. Because, once again, readers will let you know if a type of clothing is for peasants in book one but now appears on the prince in book five. Or whatever the detail may be. The more your world is real in your mind, the more real you will make it for your readers.

Description

How are your readers going to know your story world unless you tell them about it, right? Wrong. Long (or even short) amounts of description just for its own sake pulls your reader out of the emotional experience. It's like taking them aside to explain things. Again, if they are in your hero's skin, they will experience it with your hero. Reveal it like bread crumbs, just dropping a bit as it's needed. And what each character notices and experiences will vary based on who they are, giving us another layer of insight into them.

First lines

This is important to be thinking about. Once you know where to start the story, you have to start the story. First lines set the tone and create an expectation for your reader as to what's going to come next. These can take longer to craft than many of your chapters. There's more art than science to it.

Look at some of your favorite books and just read the first line. Is there something unusual, ominous, funny, or any other adjective that makes you want to keep reading? As writers, our tendency is to set the stage for what's going on. That's not as interesting. Be interesting first, then back into setting the stage as you need to.

Now that we have all of our pieces for Act I, let's move on to Act II.

Apply it!

Craft the opening scene for your book.

- What type of situation could you put her in to evoke a strong emotion in your reader?
- Make sure you include two of these qualities that evoke strong emotion: sympathetic, admirable, likable, skilled, funny, heroic, relatable.
- Did you set up the external story goal?
- Did you give a glimpse of hope?
- Did you convey the sense that all is not well, that change is coming?
- What's your inciting incident? Given her past, what event would compel her to react and begin the external goal quest?
- Did you convey the story world without an info dump?

Chapter 8
PLOTS AND SUBPLOTS

ACT II BEGINS when the hero decides to walk through the door brought about by the Inciting Incident. It's a point of no return that begins the adventure.

We already have all of the pieces we need for Act II. The Inciting Incident and the Ending are the two tent poles bracketing Act II. We know the beginning and the ending. The Backstory and the Why give us the information for Act II.

We have two big scenes already written. In Act IIA, the hero tells someone her Dark Moment story from her past. This generates empathy with the reader.

In Act IIB, she tells someone her Happiest Moment story. Now we are far enough along in the story that the hero is beginning to have a little more self-knowledge. She's beginning to see why she does what she does based on her past. And what she might need to do to change it.

Obstacles

All of the story-level obstacles we uncovered in chapter six will come into play here. They need to come from her internal emotional and psychological barriers at the root, though they can be enhanced by the various other factors we talked about such as the physical world, relationships, and institutions.

A few questions to get you thinking about powerful obstacles for Act II.

- What is she scared of?
- Why does she believe she'll fail?
- How does achieving one goal force her to abandon another goal?
- What values would achieving that goal violate and/or compromise?

Remember the four D's

This is where they come into play.

- Distancing
- Denial
- Destruction
- Devastation

How can you distance her from her goal. How can you deny her something she wants? What kind of destruction and devastation can you bring about? Remember, like with Disaster, we are more likely talking about emotional devastation and destruction than the physical version. Unless your story involves actually blowing things up. Then go with the physical destruction.

The Fight

Toward the end of Act II, we should feel the tension building as we move toward the Black Moment. Leading up to that moment is the Fight. This sometimes creates a false ending when your hero overcomes and all seems perfectly fine. But they don't see that the villain has one more battle in him.

Or it could be a false death, where it seems that all is lost and your hero should just pack it up and go, because she's not going to get what she wants. Either way, you need to give your hero a taste of death, a sense of how big the stakes really are and a feeling that she isn't going to win this battle. And a taste of victory, where it feels like, yes, they really can win this thing. Either way, it's a drive toward the Black Moment where the biggest battle will be fought.

If you use the false ending, where all seems like it's going to end well, you need to give a taste of death, a moment where it doesn't look like it's going to end well, before they get a good ending (for now).

Examples

In *Star Wars*, they escape the Death Star with the plans and return to the Rebel base after a short shoot out with the Empire. They had a taste of death, but they won and came out victorious. For now.

In *Indiana Jones and the Raiders of the Lost Ark*, the Nazis have gotten the Ark and are taking it to Petra. It seems like they have won. But Indy hid on the U-boat and followed them, driving toward the final confrontation when they open the Ark and are destroyed.

Overview

In Act II, you must balance the external, story-level elements with the internal ones.

Story-level elements:

- Disappointments
- Difficult decisions
- Competing values
- Public Stakes
- Private Stakes
- Attempt to solve the problem by cheating, but makes it worse
- Disaster
- Destruction
- Act IIA--Tells someone the Dark Moment Story
- Act IIB--Tells someone the Happiest Moment Story
- The Fight
- The taste of death
- The taste of victory
- Drive toward the Black Moment

Internal-level elements:

- Choices reveal values and Backstory
- Goals and values come into conflict

- Does something she would never do in ordinary circumstances given her Worldview and Backstory
- Sees her greatest desire
- Sees her flaw for what it is

Subplots

Subplots are a great way to add depth to your novel. They can create a complication for your character or introduce other character journeys, which is especially helpful if you are writing a series. They also help keep your plot from sagging by adding another element of story when your main story line needs a breather.

They often occur after a major twist, turning point, or revelation. This can be the plot support while our main characters take a breather. Or it can create tension by delaying information in the main plot line.

They can supply information that affects the main storyline. Especially if there isn't another good way to get it in.

It's great if you can use them to make your hero's quest harder. Imagine your main character has a difficult job to do, possibly a detective trying to solve a murder. Now add to it the subplot of trouble at home. His job makes it difficult for him to resolve the issues at home; the issues at home make it more difficult for him to do his job. See how a subplot can make things worse for our hero?

Most of all, a subplot should deepen our understanding of her. Give us a peek into another facet of her life. You can draw on some of the qualities that we introduced about her in the first chapter and continue those throughout the story. Once more, we are creating well-rounded, realistic characters that our readers can emotionally bond with.

Act III

Act III is the end we're driving for from the beginning. We've talked about knowing the ending before we begin writing so we know where we're headed. Now let's look at the components that make a strong ending.

The Black Moment

The transition from Act II to Act III is brought about by the Black Moment.

- The lie must feel real in the Black Moment, where Devastation occurs and all seems lost.
- But she realizes it isn't based on everything she's learned up to this point, all the obstacles she overcame in Act II.
- There's an Aha! moment of clarity (Epiphany) that gives her the courage and strength to engage in the "final battle."
- Her wound is healed.

Examples

In *Star Wars*, Luke can't make the drop of the bombs onto the Death Star. Everyone is going to die, and it'll be his fault. The lie seems real. This is the Dark Moment. Then he hears Obi Wan's voice in his head telling him to use the force. That is his Aha! Moment. He knows the truth. It has set him free. He turns off the instruments and uses the force to guide the bombs in, destroying the death star and saving the day. That's his final battle and victory.

In *Flash Point*, Sarah's worst fears come true when Joe is injured in a fire and she has no word from him and no idea what happened. The lie that fire will take everything precious to her seems real. But with the help of her friend, she remembers that Joe saves people. That is his calling. And good people are always needed to battle bad people, and if she gives up now, she's no better than her mother who gave up after her child died. This gives her the strength to fight an actual fire, something she couldn't do at the beginning, and help Joe save someone from a fire in the final battle.

An ending must have these elements to be satisfying.

- Happily Ever After must come true in some fashion at the end. At the beginning, we gave our hero a Glimpse of Hope that relates to her internal goal. She must achieve this to have an emotionally satisfying ending.

In *Flash Point,* Sarah's happiest moment was camping with her friend's large family. In the epilogue, she's re-created that with a large group of friends that include her and make her feel a part of something more than herself.

- The emotional satisfaction is more important than how the plot wraps up. We need the internal goal to be met, even if the external goal is not.

Sarah's external goal was to keep things steady, no changes. That does not happen. She even causes damage to the firm where she works. But her internal goal of belonging is achieved. She has a group of people that will go through life's difficult times with her and not leave her.

- The external goal does not have to be achieved. Sometimes it shows great character growth if it isn't met.
- She has to face her biggest fear (relive her Dark Moment) to experience change.

Sarah faces losing Joe to a fire, and her fear of losing someone she loves to a fire seems real.

- Her lie is proved to be a lie.

Joe not only survives, he helps people. There is a greater good that he represents, that she begins to see beyond just the threat to herself. Even better, she learns we aren't guaranteed anything regardless of our jobs, so it's important to love the people we love now.

- Her wound is visibly healed. This is often shown by the hero doing something at the end that she couldn't do at the beginning. This doesn't have to be a big thing. It could be going swimming if she was afraid of water or having a conversation that might be difficult or speaking in front of people.

In *Flash Point,* Sarah can actually confront fire and be around it in the final battle. In the epilogue, she can actually enjoy a bonfire with friends.

- Her deepest desire is reached or reachable.

Sarah has a wonderful group of friends and a man she loves who loves her.

- Her change must have been earned, not given to her. She's gone through many, many challenges to get to this point.
- She must return to where she started in the story —literally or figuratively—to show how she is different.

In *Flash Point*, the story begins and ends at the beach, but now Sarah's not alone like she was at the beginning.

Now that we've looked at the components of Act III, let's do an overview of the story-level and internal-level pieces

Overview

Story-Level

- Black Moment
- Her Dark Moment from the past resurrects itself.
- Final battle armed with truth
- Happily Ever After
- All plot threads resolved
- Circle back to the beginning (literally or figuratively) to show change.

However, if you are writing a series where the hero will appear in more than one book, it is okay to have a subplot that isn't resolved and that carries into the next book. Also, the hero will have a large, series-long arc and each book will resolve one step on his journey, bringing him closer to completeness by the final book.

The main thing is that the story goal and internal goal for this book are resolved and the major plot threads are tied up to give your reader a satisfying ending. You don't want any cliffhangers where you readers will feel manipulated.

Internal-Level

- The lie feels real
- All she has learned up until now refutes the lie
- The Aha! Moment or epiphany
- The wound is healed
- She is changed by the truth
- Her greatest dream/internal goal symbolized by the Happiest Moment are realized in some form.

And there you have it! All the pieces that you need to create an emotionally compelling story. Now, how do we get these pieces to work when it comes to actually writing them? We'll look at that next as we create page-turning scenes.

Apply it!

Sketch out the components of Act II.

Answer these questions for your main characters:

- What is she scared of?
- Why does she believe she'll fail?
- How does achieving one goal force her to abandon another goal?

- What values would achieving that goal violate and/or compromise?

Sketch out the components of Act III.

- What elements need to happen in your Black Moment? How might your hero's Dark Moment resurrect itself?
- What might her Happily Ever After look like?
- How can you circle back to the beginning literally or figuratively?

Chapter 9
PAGE-TURNING SCENES

WE'VE TALKED about the structure of the whole novel, but each scene also has its own structure that needs to be followed to ensure your readers will stay hooked turning pages.

Randy Ingermanson says actual scene construction is one of the biggest faults he sees with writers and the one change that can make the biggest difference in their writing. So we want to make sure we are constructing our scenes to be page turners.

Scene structure

A scene is the basic unit of your novel. If you use Scrivener, it is designed to take advantage of this fact. It allows you to move scenes around easily. Each act is composed of a set of scenes, which can be grouped into chapters. **Each scene should serve as a mini story.**

Action + Reaction + Decision repeated equals your plot

Your character does something or has something done to her. Then there is a reaction and a decision. That series repeated over and over becomes the narrative thread that runs through your plot. Each scene must influence the next one. The action leads to a reaction which leads to a decision which leads to another action. It should create a domino effect that is set in motion by the inciting incident and continues until the book ends. Looking back on the plot, it should make perfect sense.

The why of each action, reaction, and decision must make sense given her world view and backstory. But we only want to give the reader as much info as they need right now in this scene.

And nothing else belongs on the page. Let's dig in to the particulars of what will make up these Actions, Reactions, and Decisions.

A scene:

- Is a chapter or part of a chapter
- Is presented from one character's POV—this is important!
- Can be either an Action scene or a Reaction scene
- Must move the plot thread forward.
- Must have a goal (what does she want?)
- Must have a cause and effect
- Must matter (what will it cost her?)
- Must have her realize something
- Needs to end in some sort of hook to keep readers turning pages. And now? So what must happen next?
- Must create a compelling emotional experience in some way

One POV per scene

If you use more than one POV per scene, it is called head hopping. It doesn't create an emotional experience for the reader. When you maintain one POV per scene, it allows your reader to fully get into the character's skin. If you yank the reader out of that and pop them into another character, it gets confusing. And generally it means you have not used deep POV but something closer to omniscient. We'll talk more about POV in a later chapter. For here, remember that it's one POV per scene.

Action and Reaction

Yes, it's confusing terminology. You'd think a creative person would have come up with something better. This is based on Dwight Swain's *Techniques of the Selling Writer,* though Randy Ingermanson has done a wonderful job of making it more understandable in his book, *How to Write a Dynamite Scene.*

An Action scene has three components:

- Goal
- Conflict
- Disaster (Which naturally leads into the Reaction to the Disaster)

A Reaction scene has three components:

- Reaction
- Dilemma

- Decision (Done correctly, this will also create a hook.)

Let's examine these a bit more in depth.

Goal

We talked early about story-level goals. Now we are talking about scene-level goals. What does your POV character want at the beginning of the scene? This can be thought of as the sub-goals that make up the bigger, story-level goal. But each scene does need to have a goal. Otherwise, what is the purpose of it?

Notice I said POV character. Depending on the scene and how many POV characters you have, this could be the hero, the love interest, the villain, and so on. Whoever it is, this is their scene. What do they want? Establishing this early in the scene. Even the first sentence!

You need a goal to keep your scene moving the plot forward and to make your character proactive. Nobody likes a hero who waits to get rescued. No one finds it interesting when things just "happen" to work out. Even when our villains have goals, it makes us more emotionally engaged because now we're afraid for the hero.

The more desperately a character wants something, the more interesting and emotionally involving the scene becomes.

A goal should be:

- Possible. If they can't achieve it, then what's the point? The reader will know that it's doomed.
- Difficult. The value comes from the struggle. It should be possible but not easy. Otherwise how will our character grow?

- Fit the character's backstory and worldview
- Concrete and objective. We know what the goal is and can tell whether she's reached it or not.
- Be the most important thing in your character's life right now at this moment. That creates a sense of urgency and necessity. Now sometimes it could be as simple as getting across the room on crutches to get a glass of water. Or it could be saving someone's life. It's what's most important in that particular moment.

Examples

Star Wars. Luke and Han have rescued Princess Leia, but they are still on the Death Star. Their Goal is to return to Han's ship and escape.

Coming Home. Becca wants to get through her brother's funeral without having an embarrassing conversation with his best friend, Seth.

Conflict

And just as there are story- and scene-level goals, there are also story- and scene-level conflict. Just like with the goals, the scene-level conflict can be the smaller conflicts or pieces of conflict that make up the larger, story-level conflict.

As with story-level conflict, this is not just about fighting or arguing. As I've said, I really think the better term is *obstacle*, for it's really the series of obstacles that stand in the way of your POV character getting the Goal of the scene that we just determined in the previous step. You can also think of it as resistance to getting her goal.

You must have an obstacle or a struggle. If your POV character gets what she wants out of the scene without conflict, that's boring and not emotionally engaging. The value comes from the struggle. The bigger the goal, the bigger the struggle.

Think back to our brain science. The brain wants to thrive and survive, and it's looking to your story to tell it how to do that. But if there is no struggle, then the brain doesn't get the info it's looking for. It knows there are going to be struggles and obstacles in life, and it is looking to your book to tell it how to overcome them. So make your reader's brain happy and give the brain what it wants.

In a scene, the conflict should:

- Be a series of actions and reactions repeated until there is a disaster.
- Be most of the scene. Otherwise, why is it there?
- Test our POV character and put the outcome in question, not be easily overcome.
- Be as big as the stakes. The bigger the stakes, the longer the scene.
- Impact either the internal or external goals of the character.
- Connect with the reader.
- Produce emotion.

Let's review the kinds of conflict. These can work for story-level conflict and scene-level conflict.

The conflict can be:

. . .

Inherent conflicts in plot:

- Setting: distance in relationships, bad memories, dangerous environment
- Opponents: different viewpoints, opposing desires and wants
- Relationships: mother and daughter, romantic, siblings, coworkers, etc.

External Conflict

- Outside world pressing in
- Two or more people whose needs or wants are in competition

However, when creating external conflict, the most successful ones are those that:

- Exacerbate your main character's internal conflict.
- Can be symbolized by a concrete obstacle

Internal Conflict

- Personal issues — doubts, fears, internal turmoil
- Two opposing desires
- Protection against something
- Spiritual, existential struggle
- Major flaw

Example

Star Wars. Storm troopers guard the ship, blocking Luke, Han, and Leia. Darth Vader is approaching, and only Obi-wan Kenobi blocks him.

Coming Home. Seth comes out to the porch where Becca has escaped to from the funeral. She's been avoiding him, but now she's trapped. She thinks they are going to have that embarrassing conversation.

A well-written conflict should lead to . . . Disaster.

The Disaster

Your POV character fails to reach her Goal. It can be as large as a disaster or simply a setback. What a huge let down! We wanted her to win. There can be small victories in the story, but either they are not enough or they don't turn out to be what the hero thought they would be. He gets his wish, but he wishes he didn't. Or it turns out to be only a small reprieve in the big scheme of things.

When bad things happen, readers keep turning pages to see what happens next. Who can put a book down when things are going badly? Disaster, like Conflict, creates an emotionally compelling read.

We don't want to see the hero fail. In fact, her failure to get her goal creates an open loop in the reader's mind, and they will want to keep reading to see if she does get her Goal somewhere down the line. This is why a victory will close the loop unless it somehow doesn't or immediately opens another loop. This is also brain science, and it's called the Zeigarnik Effect. The brain keeps working on a problem until it's solved, even if you walk away, which is why you get brilliant ideas in the shower, on a walk, or in the middle of the night.

A Disaster:

- Closes out the scene and creates a hook.
- Is the opposite (even if it's the emotional opposite) of the goal.
- Leaves your POV character worse off than they were at the beginning of the scene.
- Should force the reader to turn the page to see what happens next.
- Should be emotionally powerful (but perhaps not emotionally satisfying).

The Disaster can be found by asking:

- What is the worst thing, externally (circumstance or physically), that could happen to my character?
- How could I ruin her life right now?
- What is my character's worst fear at the moment?
- What is the worst information my character can receive right now?
- What is the worst trouble my character can get into in this scene? Raise the stakes so that they are further from their overall goals.
- Have I set up the danger for the readers before the scene begins (unexpected yet plausible)?
- Have I made my reader care about my character? Can they sympathize? Spell out the stakes often enough so the reader worries!

Even when she gets what she wants or it looks like a good thing has happened, it should still raise the question in the readers mind, "So now what?" and keep them turning pages. Readers constantly need to be waiting for the other shoe to drop.

Examples

> *Star Wars.* Darth Vader kills Obi-wan Kenobi, distracting the Storm Troopers and allowing Luke, Han, and Leia to escape.

This is an interesting point to note. Because this is a movie, it's hard to say who the POV character is. But if you go back to the goal, you'll see it's for Luke, Han, and Leia to escape. Technically, they do escape and meet their goal. But at what cost? They've lost the mentor of the group, the only one who knew how to guide them. This is an example of getting what they want, but then wishing they hadn't.

> *Coming Home.* Seth doesn't bring up the embarrassing subject. He talks about something worse, her brother's death. She turns into a sobbing mess, something that only reinforces his image of her as an emotional child.

Even if there is a small victory with the Goal, this victory must launch a new set of obstacles, even worse than before. So, in the end, your character is in a worse place.

Now, these sound like grand, sweeping terms. But remember Disaster, Destruction, something she would never do are all emotional barometers. They are all very personal to your POV character.

Whew! That's exhausting. That's why we need a break.

And so do our readers. So following an Action scene, we need a Reaction scene to give us a moment to digest what happened and to catch our breath.

Reaction scene

A Reaction scene is:

- Reaction (emotions and then thoughts)
- Dilemma
- Decision

Digging deeper . . .

Reaction

A Reaction is an **emotional** result of the Disaster. Give your character and the reader a bit of time to feel the emotions and how long it takes to process them. This will vary based on the extent of the Disaster. Because this is internal, you might have more telling here. Still, tread lightly.

Resist the urge to be the writer telling us what the hero is doing. Let us into her skin so we know her thoughts and feelings. Give your readers an emotionally compelling read. This is a great place to use a friend or a mentor character to bounce emotions off of. You will have dialogue if the POV character is talking things over with someone else or interior monologue if she is ruminating on the choices by herself.

A Reaction scene is compelling because there is always the temptation for your hero to give up. We all know life is hard and bad things happen. But we admire the people who don't give up. The reader's brain is looking for that secret. What keeps your hero going when life gets rough?

A story isn't what happens, it's how your hero **reacts** to what happens.

- Show her train of thought as she reacts to everything.
- Show her figuring out how to deal with the latest action.
- Show her figuring out how to still achieve her goals.
- Show the "why" as she is figuring it out.

Margie Lawson's classes are particularly helpful here (see the Resources section).

Remember this, people react first, and then think through things more logically. But **the emotional reaction always comes first.** The reaction should be in line with your character's goals, values, backstory, and worldview.

Examples

Star Wars. Luke is grieving Obi-wan Kenobi after they've escaped from the Death Star. He does not know what to do next, because now his mentor is dead, and he's not used to making decisions. He talks about it with Leia.

Coming Home. Becca feels the tug to stay in Reedsville instead of returning to school. But school represents all she's ever wanted. But Reedsville represents the family and sense of belonging she's always wanted. She talks about her brother's death with Maggie then heads outside to revisit their favorite places.

Dilemma

When your character begins to get a grip on her emotions and tries to decide what to do, there she sees her Dilemma. She has no good options. When you set up your Disaster, try to eliminate as many options as possible to set up the Dilemma. Your reader needs to worry and wonder how the POV character can possibly get out of this mess. Let your hero work through the choices until she comes to the least-bad one.

In contrast to the emotion of the Reaction, the Dilemma is more **logical** and **intellectual**. It should highlight the POV character's ability to think rationally. If something about the Disaster ruined her ability to think rationally, she just might make the mess worse (yay!).

Decision

This allows your POV character to become proactive again. They can't wait for someone else to decide, they need to act. Also don't let them dither around too long. No one wants to read about that. Right or wrong, they need to make a decision and act on it. It has to have some reasonable basis in the character's values and what we know about her to this point.

A Decision can come about by accident, but don't make it a hand-of-God thing that makes it feel like the writer is manipulating things. The Decision can involve intellect or emotion.

The brain is also engaged here as well. We often put off decisions, because decisions are hard. We admire people who make hard decisions. And the brain wants to learn how to do this, so it will be engaged while your hero is going through the decision-making process.

Because of their lower tension, Reaction scenes tend to

be shorter. You can show a full Reaction scene. You can tell it briefly as part of the next Action scene. Or you can skip it and see if your reader can figure out what happened between the two Action scenes. This makes the most sense in a series of heavy action scenes without a lot of time for reflective thought. Even if you don't put it on the page, you should still know your hero's Reaction, Dilemma, and Decision.

Now your character's Decision has become her new Goal (see how that works?). Make sure that it follows all the same criteria for a Goal that we've previously discussed.

Examples

In *Star Wars*, Imperial fighters come after the ship, forcing Luke to snap out of it and help defend himself and the others. His new goal is to survive the battle and be part of a new team.

In *Coming Home*, Becca decides to keep with her original plan to return to school in a week. Her goal is the same, with a twist: to get through the week, but to get Seth to see her as a capable, modern woman.

Now we've gone full circle from Action to Reaction to Action again. This continues until you have the hero triumph in victory or go down in defeat. This creates an emotionally compelling reading experience that keeps your readers turning pages because there's no good place to stop.

Scene turning points

Scene turning points can happen in either the Action or the Reaction scene. They often are a result of lies, secrets, misbeliefs, or revelations. Mine the past (there's that backstory again) for people, conflicts, sources of misbeliefs. Any time you can make things take a sharp, unexpected turn, you're engaging your reader.

One more point

You know that old writing advice "write what you know"? Which is total bunk. If that was true, we'd write pretty narrow stories. But I would say, in the words of Lisa Cron, "Write what you know… emotionally." Use your emotions and emotional experiences to pull from and infuse your characters with realism and create an emotionally-compelling read.

Tension

All along we've been talking about how we want stories rich in conflict. By adding tension, we're making the conflict even richer. Tension is conflict with emotion.

For each scene, whether it's an Action scene or a Reaction scene, ask yourself how you can infuse more emotion into the conflict. Here are some ideas.

- Reveal something previously unknown
- Create a question for the reader
- Show conflicting feelings and ideas. This works well in the Dilemma portion of a Reaction scene
- Mine the past for problems that come back up
- Show competing internal desires. This is similar to the competing values we talked about earlier.
- When you have clashing personalities, go deeper to differing values and morals.

You can use the writing itself to create tension. At a larger level, how you intersperse your Action and Reaction scenes can affect tension. Shorter scenes create a greater sense of tension. A longer Action scene and a shorter or non-existent Reaction scenes quickens the pace. A longer Reaction scene slows it down. Play with that to draw out the tension.

The same is also true at the sentence level. Shorter, choppier sentences with strong, active verbs create a sense of action and movement. Choose short, hard-edged words to convey this as well. Longer sentences, especially with "ing" verbs that indicated continuing action convey a more leisurely pace.

Now, you might think you always want a fast pace to keep readers turning pages. But not necessarily so. Think of this scenario. You have an Action scene. Your POV character is tied to the railroad tracks, in danger of an on-coming train. Then, you cut to the hero's POV, and this is a more leisurely scene. He has no idea about the danger the other character is in. He's drinking coffee and talking to the neighbors. The writing has longer sentences and words. But you the reader know about the danger the other character is in, and it's driving you nuts that he's not dashing out to save her. Is that tension? You bet.

Another great technique is to cut a scene in the middle of the action. That can really keep your readers on edge as they have to keep reading to see what happens. You can also create a distraction, something that pops up that hasn't been part of the scene up to this point.

Make the most of your story's "big" scenes. Scenes that are major turning points require more space than other scenes if they're to develop to a satisfying emotional peak. In scenes involving important turning points, revelations, pivotal action, try to:

1. Draw out the moment leading up to the pivotal action or revelation. Let the reader savor the anticipation before you deliver the goods. Let the reader experience the full emotional impact of each major plot event.

2. As the writer, you must know all the actions, reactions, and motivations of the characters in the scene. Use this to create more tension. But don't change point-of-view in order to do this or you will inadvertently diffuse the building tension of the scene by head hopping. More on this in chapter 12.

3. Moments of high tension require precise verbs, terse writing, shorter sentences and paragraphs than usual. Go to one of your favorite suspense novels and re-read the concluding chapters. Compare a page of highly intense conflict with one of the earlier pages in the book. Can you spot the differences?

4. Focusing on small details can be more effective than comprehensive, full-blown descriptions. For example, during a reading-of-the-will scene, rather than describing the library or the clothing of the participants, focus on one small, telling detail—say the old-fashioned clock sitting on the dead man's desk, which is now stopped since he hasn't wound it.

5. Just as you draw out the moments preceding the pivotal action, you exit quickly once the high note has been achieved. If it is necessary to tie up loose ends, do this in another scene, perhaps through a different point-of-view character or through a Reaction scene.

Don't weigh down your pivotal scenes with too much reflection or narrative. The high-tension moments of your story are not the times to be going into flashback mode or to be filling in holes in the character's back story. In these scenes, even more than any other, it is important to keep your writing active and focused on what is happening at that moment in time. This is where following the Action scene sequence of Goal-Conflict-Disaster will help keep you on track.

Prewriting

Prewriting is one of the best ways to beat writer's block and to ensure that your scene has all of the great components it needs before you even get writing it. It's also a way to write more quickly, because when you know what a scene is going to be about, it's easier to see it play out in your head and then you are nearly transcribing what you are seeing.

Before I write a scene, I make some notes in the Document Notes section of my scene in Scrivener. Here are the questions I want to answer before I write the scene:

- Who's POV is it?
- What is their goal for this scene? How can I create obstacles or disasters for that?
- Who else might be in the scene or needs to be in the scene?
- Is this an Action scene or a Reaction scene?
- What could be some potential Goal/Conflict/Disaster (Action scene) or the Reaction/Dilemma/Decision (Reaction scene)?

- What's come before that needs to be addressed, like a decision or a disaster?
- What are we heading toward next that we need to be setting up now?
- How does this go to the emotional wound/lie of the POV character?
- Sketch out how the dialogue might go (We'll talk about dialogue in chapter 11). What is each person's agenda? Subtext? Body language?

As you can see, by starting to ask these questions, you move right into creative brain, drawing on all the work you've already done. It ensures that you are writing relevant scenes that pull the reader through the story and create a compelling emotional experience.

Apply it!

- Write four scenes. Two should be Action scenes (Goal/Conflict/Disaster) and two should be Reaction scenes (Reaction/Dilemma/Decision).
- Use the prewriting technique to sketch out your scenes in advance.
- Bonus: keep writing until the structure begins to feel natural.

Chapter 10

THE SMALL PICTURE: STIMULUS AND RESPONSE

DWIGHT SWAIN in *Techniques of the Selling Writer* origi-nally used the term MRU—motivation reaction unit. It sounded icky and stuffy, so with the help of one of my students, Tracy Borgmeyer, we came up with a better term: Stimulus Response Units. The point is really not what we call them, but to remember that every action has a reaction, and they need to come in the proper order to feel natural and realistic.

Let's go back to the last chapter on Action and Reaction scenes and let's start with a Reaction scene. It needs to follow the Reaction/Dilemma/Decision pattern. If our hero came to a decision before we even knew what the dilemma was, the scene would feel disjointed and not have the same emotional impact. Reaction/Dilemma/Decision follows a particular order because that's how we actually process information in the real world, and if our characters do it differently, it pulls us out of the story.

The same is true for every action that happens in the story. Its reaction needs to occur *after* the action, and needs to be the right kind of reaction. Let's unpack this.

First, just like Action and Reaction applies to whomever is the POV character, the same is true for Stimulus Response Units. They are based on the POV character and what they can see, experience, and feel.

There are two parts to keep straight. Stimulus and Response

Stimulus is what your POV character sees. It is external and could be seen by anyone.

If a camera was filming the scene, it would be visible or audible.

Example: There's a knock at the door.

Anyone can hear that knock. There's no question or interpretation needed.

Response is what your POV character does in response to the Stimulus.

It is internal and subjective. And it occurs in a physiologically precise order.

1. Instinct and feelings
2. Reflexive actions
3. Rational actions and speech

Example: There's a knock at the door. Joe jumps and his heart pounds (1). He leaps from the couch (2). Could Marie be at the door? How did she get here so quickly? He peeks out the window (3).

When you read it, it makes perfect sense. You can see it

playing out. But if we move the pieces around, it just seems wrong.

> He leaps from the couch. There's a knock at the door. He peeks out the window. Could Marie be at the door? How did she get here so quickly? Joe jumps and his heart pounds.

I've seen sentences like that and so have you. But it doesn't feel right. It feels jerky, and it keeps your reader from getting in emotionally deep with the characters, which is the only reason we do anything! You lose the emotional reaction of the reader because there is nothing to respond to. The Response is where the emotionally compelling part is. Get us in your POV character's skin and let us react to the Stimulus exactly like your character would react.

The Response will vary based on your POV character and their backstory

It all comes around to backstory, doesn't it? Look at this example with the same Stimulus.

> There's a knock at the door. Joe's heart pounds, a grin spreading across his face. He leaps up. Could Marie be at the door so quickly with his birthday present? He flings open the door.

A knock at the door could mean something good or something bad depending on your character. But notice that the order of the Response stayed the same.

. . .

Not every step of the Response must be included, but those that are must be in the proper order.

There's a knock at the door. Joe leaps up. Could Marie be at the door so quickly with his birthday present?

Here it is the wrong way:

There's a knock at the door. Could Marie be at the door so quickly with his birthday present? Joe leaps up.

It just feels wrong, like a campy *SNL* skit.

The final Response step will lead to a new Stimulus and the cycle continues.

Just as how Goal/Conflict/Disaster leads to Reaction/Dilemma/Decision leads to Goal/Conflict/Disaster, the Stimulus Response cycle also repeats itself. This will help you in your prewriting because you can sketch out the medium picture (GCD or RDD) and then within that you can sketch out your Stimulus Responses. When you do your actual writing of the scene, you'll know what your characters need to do already.

There's a knock at the door. Joe's heart pounds, a grin spreading across his face. He leaps up. Could Marie be at the door so quickly with his birthday present? He flings open the door. (First Stimulus Response set.)

Marie stands there with a present in her hands (objective Stimulus). Joe smiles. He hopes it's the new video game he wants. He reaches for the present. "Won't you come in?" (Subjective Response, second Stimulus Response set.)

Continue alternating Stimulus Responses as you work through the Goal/Conflict/Disaster or Reaction/Dilemma/Decision.

Let's look at a real example to show you how this works. This is the prologue to *Coming Home*. It is a **Goal/Conflict/Disaster** scene.

"Watch out!" (This is the **Stimulus**. The *Goal* of the scene is to get a section logged without anyone getting hurt. It's not explicitly stated, but it becomes the obvious motivation of Thomas during this scene.)

Furious, Thomas Wilson hauled the careless man back. He'd come within an inch of being whacked by a whip saw. Thomas released him with a glare. (**Response**. *Furious* is internal and reflexive, step 2, skipping step 1. The next sentence is logical thought, step 3, and logical action. *Conflict*—the man's actions threaten Thomas's goal)

The man's gaze drifted to the saw. A near miss. Eyes round, he stumbled away across the uneven ground. (**Response**, this time by the man who nearly got hit. He's not our POV character so we have to be careful that what we show is what Thomas, our POV character, can see. We can see someone else's reaction, which is obvious by his widened eyes, step 2, and stumbling away, step 3.)

Thomas inwardly groaned and ran his hand through his hair. This new man was particularly careless. Maybe he should fire him before he got himself killed. The safety of their men had always been a priority for Thomas and his partner Seth, which made them different from other outfits. He held his beliefs private, but he reckoned men were more productive when you treated them like men instead of animals. Of course with some outfits using steam engines and locomotives for logging, there might not be logging much longer—for men or beasts.

(**Response**. Thomas's actions are still in reaction to the man who almost got killed. This is a complex reaction because now we are past the first emotion of it, it leads to his train of thought. *Goal* is reiterated.)

Normally being out among the trees was the best part of Thomas's day. The scent of pine and fresh wood chips with the forest floor crisp under his boots beat doing paperwork at his desk any day. Seth caught that chore today. Though now he wondered who had the better deal. (**Response**. *Normally, this is great but the doofus who almost died is ruining today. Conflict*—man's actions have ruined Thomas's enjoyment of the day.)

Thomas figured he and Seth wouldn't have to try to make a success at this business much longer. In fact, what might be the perfect opportunity to get out of logging all together lay in a letter on his desk. On top of that, once his little sister, Becca, graduated from the University down in Salem and got herself married off, Thomas wouldn't have her to worry about. (New **Stimulus**. He wouldn't have to worry about doofuses much longer because he has this letter, his new motivation, and his sister is graduating, yet another motivation. **Response** is just step 3, rational thought. *New goal*—get out of this business and see Becca taken care of.)

Then whatever he turned his hand to wouldn't matter so much. It'd just been him and Becca for the past ten years, and he'd done a fair job of caring for her. Hopefully, that time was drawing to a close. She could be a handful at times, and he'd be more than happy to turn her over to the right man who could handle her.

Raised voices carried through the air, yanking him out of his thoughts. He jerked his head up, and he listened to the commotion that brewed between his men. He jogged over. (**Stimulus**—raised voices. **Response** starting at step

2, reflexive—yanking, jerked— then to step three, rational action. *Conflict*—the trees are rotten.)

"This has conk rot," a logger yelled from the top of a tree. "It's no good. Check the others." (New **Stimulus**.)

Thomas groaned again. This day was souring fast, like left-out milk. Seth definitely had the better draw today. (**Response**.)

"Look out!" (**Stimulus**)

He spun just in time to see a log break free of its chains and barrel downhill. (**Response**)

The new man stood dead center in the path of the runaway log, back turned. (**Stimulus**)

Sprinting at full speed, Thomas plowed into him, tumbling him out of the way. Sprawled on the ground. Tried to scramble to his feet. (**Response**)

Something grabbed at him. He looked down to see his leg tangled in tree branches the men hadn't yet cleared. (**Stimulus**—something grabbed him. **Response**—looked down, reveals a new **Stimulus**—tangled branches. New *Goal*—save the new guy. *Conflict*—Now Thomas is tangled.)

Panic shot through him. He kicked. And kicked again. The branches cinched around his legs like a noose. He'd need to be cut out. (**Response**. All three steps. Instinct, reflex, logical thought. New *Goal*—save himself.)

But there wasn't time.

The roar in his ears told him it was too late.

Dear God, Becca . . . was his last thought before all went black. (**Disaster**—he didn't save himself and he can't help Becca.)

See how the Stimulus and Response got simpler, faster, and closer together as the action peaked? Using this progression correctly helps with the pace of your story.

Now let's look at it with a **Reaction/Dilemma/Decision** scene. This one is interesting in that Seth is reacting to Becca's arrival in Reedsville, but he didn't have a Goal/Conflict/Disaster scene in his POV first.

Seth splashed water on his face. (**Stimulus**—objective, visual. This is a *Reaction* scene, and he is reacting to seeing Becca come back to town.

Was he dreaming? The beautiful young woman Maggie brought into her house bore very little resemblance to the awkward, gangly girl who'd left. (**Response**—rational thought, step 3. But we also know that Seth is splashing water on his face in response to the emotions he felt at seeing Becca. It's implied but because we are tied into his emotions, we know intrinsically the emotions behind his actions without the writer having to spell them out. Besides, Seth is a guy, so he's not likely to even know what his emotions are. :))

When Becca stepped off the stage, her clothes were dusty and wrinkled, and there was a hardness to the light in her green eyes. But the sunlight hit her hair, making it gleam like polished gold. (Seth is recalling a memory, as part of his *Reaction* scene. It provides a **Stimulus**.)

Fascinated by her smooth skin and full lips, he hadn't even recognized her! The old tintype photograph on Thomas's desk at the logging camp didn't do her justice. What happened to the girl he'd once called his Li'l Sis? (His **Response** to seeing her, emotional then logical. The Response continues below in his reminiscing about their shared past. Also a *Dilemma*—she's not who he remembered her to be. Now what?)

When they were much younger, she'd beg to go on adventures with Thomas and him, and usually he was the one to give in. Without siblings or a mother, Seth found

Becca to be somewhere between a curiosity and a nuisance when he wanted to go fish with Thomas. Braids flying, freckles dotting her nose and cheeks, all elbows and knees, determined to keep up with the boys.

Running the linen cloth over his face, he grinned remembering Becca throwing herself in his arms, whispering she loved him. She'd spun around and jumped on the stage without hearing his reply. (This is a new **Stimulus** because it's a physical action in the present that's objective. We can see him doing this. While we can't see him remembering, what he is remembering is something that we could see. This memory provides the **Stimulus** for what happens next. Also a **Response** to his thoughts about their shared past.)

He'd repeated that scene many times in his mind since she left, touched she'd thought of him as another big brother. (This is interesting because his **Response** in the past creates his **Stimulus** in the present.)

He sobered at the thought. It was his fault her real brother was dead. Up until he left the logging camp to meet her stage he'd thought Thomas's death was an accident. (His **Response** is this whole paragraph. Emotions, then rational thought. Which also presents a *Dilemma*.)

But Owen Taylor had stopped him, coming out of the logging camp office carrying a pile of chains. "Hey, Seth, I've been thinking about… well, you know, the accident. And I remembered one fellow saying how eerie it was the way the chain broke. I didn't think much of it at the time —you know how riled up about ghosts and such some men can be—but I went to the tool barn to see if I could find the chain. Sure enough, it was sittin' there in a pile." He held out a rust-flecked chain and pointed to a link. "Look at this." (Even though this was in the past and is in

Seth's memory, when it happened it was visual and could have been seen. It provides **Stimulus** for what happens next.)

Seth lifted his hat and resettled it on his head. He didn't have time for this if he was going to meet Becca's stage. He should have left before now. (**Response**. Emotion and rational thought. His emotions being conveyed by his actions. He resettles his hat because he's annoyed and trying not to show it.)

The chain in Taylor's hands looked like one of many. He eyed the links. What made this one so special?

Then he spotted it. The one link, pulled open like an ugly mouth. (Both paragraphs are **Stimulus**. Objective. Anyone could see the chain. Seth's commentary about the "ugly mouth" gives us a clue to his **Response** which happens next. To be pure, I could have just left off the ugly mouth commentary and added it to Seth's reaction later.)

His stomach dropped, his head spun, and bile rose in his throat. He swallowed hard. It was his fault. He'd made the mistake and that chain, that link, proved it.

Grabbing Owen by the shoulder, he shoved him back into the office. "Leave that here. Don't put it back in the barn, you hear me? And make sure nothing happens to it." (Both paragraphs are **Response**— emotion and rational thought.)

Owen nodded slowly, his eyes round with surprise. "Sure, Boss. Anything you want." He tossed the chain into the corner behind Seth's desk, the clanking links sounding oddly like a death rattle. (**Stimulus**. Objective.)

Seth gave him a terse nod and strode out the door, rounding the building and heading for the outhouse. He stared at it for a moment before hauling back and slamming his fist into the door. (**Response**. Seth conveys emotion with the terse nod and punching the door—rational action? For a man. :) *Reaction* to the *Dilemma*.)

The door bounced front and back a few times before giving a groan and swinging lazily from one hinge. (**Stimulus**. Objective.)

He'd have to fix that tomorrow.

His fist stung at the memory. He glanced at the red scraped knuckles. Though injuries weren't uncommon to him, he'd keep his hand out of Maggie's sight or she'd want to doctor it. And he didn't want to explain how he got it. (**Response**. Logical thought about fixing the door, fist stings, has to hide it from Maggie. All are his thoughts.)

He tossed the towel on the hook. Her brother was dead, and he was responsible. He had to look after her; Thomas would have expected it. (Back in the present, the towel tossing is objective, so it's technically a **Stimulus**. It serves more as an action beat to break up a long **Response**. He's still Responding to the memory, and it provides the **Stimulus** for what he does next.)

Seth headed into the dining room. (**Stimulus**. Objective action.)

To a woman he didn't know and a responsibility he didn't know how to fulfill. (**Response**. Logical thought. And finally, his *Decision*.)

Showing and telling with stimulus response

The cool thing about nailing the Stimulus Response sequence is that it keeps showing and telling in their proper places, and it keeps your POV straight. If your scenes aren't behaving, check those two areas to see where something has slipped.

We know now that the Stimulus has to be showing. It has to be something we can all see. The Response is where it sometimes gets dicey. It can be easy to slip into telling, where we start telling what the POV character is thinking and feeling. Better to get us into those three steps of a Reaction scene and let us *feel* what he's feeling. Let us see the world from behind her eyes.

It is important to the emotional depth of the scene to keep it in one POV. If we are jumping from one person's reaction to another, we break the chain of Stimulus Response. We can *show* a non-POV character's reaction through the eyes of the POV character. See what we did above in the first scene with the new guy. Thomas sees the guy's eyes get wide and sees him stumble away. We infer the rest of what then new guy must be feeling, but we can't hop into his head and feel it. That would be bad. Don't do it.

Fine tuning

When you are writing, start a new paragraph every time you switch between a Stimulus and a Response. There's one place in the example above where I didn't do that. Can you find it? Separating them makes them easier to identify when you are in your analysis phase of writing.

Additionally, it first shows the action (Stimulus) through the POV character's eyes. Then it gives their Response, which is subjective and lets us in on her feelings and thoughts. This helps us dig in and feel close to the character. It creates that compelling emotional experience we are going for.

And if your lines aren't a Stimulus or a Response, you know you have to delete them. They don't move the plot forward.

Danger ahead

The danger, as I mentioned in the beginning, is letting all of this give you a bad case of writer's block. That happens when the editorial and creative departments of your brain mingle. Prewriting helps with this. Prewriting lets the editorial department do its planning. But then it needs to leave. Write the scene without analyzing it. Just create. And when you're done, go back and analyze it to see if it meets the flow and structure that it needs to. But don't think about that while you are actually writing. Prewriting should give you enough structure to free up the creative department to write and to tell the editorial department to shut up.

This lesson brings to a close the heavy lifting part of your writing. We've discussed the big, medium, and small picture structure that your scenes need. We've talked about characters and back story. You have everything you need to begin writing your novel. Yay! The rest of the lessons will be more about fine tuning and subtle things that will take your work from good to great. Don't be scared; this is where the fun begins!

Apply it!

Write four scenes (you can use the ones from the previous chapter or write new ones). Two should be Goal/Conflict/Disaster and two should be Reaction/Dilemma/Decision. Layer in the Stimulus Response sequence. Use prewriting to help you plan and then forget about the rules while you actually write.

- Go back to your scenes and color code them so you can see the Stimulus Response and the GCD or RDD.
- Edit where needed to make your scenes fit the structure.
- Bonus: keep writing until the structure begins to feel natural.

Chapter 11

DIALOGUE

AT THIS POINT, you may feel like your brain is mush and you can't put anything else in it. That's perfectly normal. You have everything you need to get writing. And most of these lessons won't really sink in until you put them into practice. Your main goal is to write, turn off the internal editor, and know that the first draft will be crummy, and that's okay. As someone once said, all a first draft has to do is exist.

There is a lot more to learn about writing a novel. It's a never-ending journey, and you will learn more with each novel that you write. And right now, we are going to learn about our characters by what they say (dialogue) and what they think (interior or internal monologue).

Dialogue is NOT supposed to be "just like real conversation." Most "real conversation" is boring and tries to avoid conflict, the opposite of what we want to accomplish on the page.

Dialogue:

- Should create an illusion of a conversation
- Must advance the plot

- Should reveal the characters by:
- Word choices and grammar. This can reveal educational level and where they are from geographically (Do they say soda or pop?). Pet phrases come into play here.
- Tone of voice. "I'd like a sandwich, please" versus "Fix me a sandwich."
- What is said and what isn't said.
- How they sound different from each other.
- How they respond and interact with each other.
- Can explain the Story World, but avoid, "As you know, Bob…" (we'll touch on this later).
- Can reveal backstory, but don't tell her life story. As we've said all along, no info dumps.
- May even expound the Theme, but don't preach (we'll touch on this later).
- Isn't always the truth. Characters lie, say what they think others want to hear, or say what they'd really like to believe is true.
- The juxtaposition of dialogue and internal monologue can deepen our connection to the hero and reveal his character by letting us in on his thoughts and how they are different from what he is saying.

Dialogue will play out a bit differently depending on the type of scene we are in.

Dialogue in an Action scene

- Each person has a different Goal.
- As a result, the dialogue reveals Conflict. It could be a battle of words or with subtexting (more to

come on that), a battle of wits—see *Pride and Prejudice* by Jane Austen. We might also get a peek into the feelings and thoughts of the POV character.

- It can show that information has been withheld, show opposition, create doubt.
- Each piece of each Stimulus Response contains rational speech.
- There may be some interior monologue, but it is limited to the POV character (no head-hopping).
- This Conflict rises in intensity to a Disaster.

Dialogue in a Reaction scene

- At least one person, for sure the POV person, has an emotional Reaction. The dialogue should reflect this.
- That person moves into a Dilemma. This is the dialogue that discusses what to do.
- There may be more internal dialogue.
- That person ends with a Decision, which is the dialogue that shows what the POV character is going to do and sets up the Goal for the next Action scene.

Prewrite your dialogue

As you sketch out your scene, deciding if it's an Action scene or Reaction scene, think about what kind of dialogue would happen.

- What is the point of the scene? What's the Disaster or Dilemma? What are you showing or trying to prove in this scene? Why does it exist?
- What is the agenda of each person in the conversation?
- Do they get what they want out of it?
- Does the other person believe what they are saying? Why or why not?
- What is the body language of each person conveying, and is it different than what the words are conveying?

That all is fairly obvious and might even make it sound more complicated than it actually is. But hang with me because there are a few ground rules we need to go over concerning dialogue.

Basic dialogue rules

- Every time a new person speaks (or thinks or reacts), they get a new paragraph. Pretty much one paragraph per person.
- Use quotation marks to set off the things people say.
- Be judicious in the use of adverbs and adjectives (she said longingly, she said compassionately) in dialogue tags. They can be distracting. Use body language, internal thought, and context to let the reader know what's going on in the scene. If all else fails, use "said," which is invisible to readers. More on this in Action Beats.
- Know the rules about which punctuation goes in or out of quotation marks.

- Put thoughts in italics but not in quotation marks. If someone says, "I'm so happy to see you!" but they are thinking *You dirty rat* while they say it, that would look like this:
- "I'm so happy to see you!" I said. *You dirty rat.* However, in Deep POV, the italics will be limited because we are already in the character's head. Use italics only for a direct thought. Every time you use italics you are reminding the reader that they aren't really in the character's head, so we want to do that as little as possible.
- Example: "I'm so happy to see you!" *You dirty rat!*
- Or "I'm so happy to see you!" That dirty rat.

Pro tip

Read your dialogue out loud. Even though it's not "real," it should still sound real and flow well.

Action beats: beyond he said, she said

Action tags or beats reveal character. They can do double or triple duty in revealing your character's emotions, thoughts, subtext, and story world. Here are a few examples of how the action beats change the meaning of the dialogue.

- "No way!" Mary slammed the files on the desk. "I can't believe you got the job."
- "No way!" Joe high-fived Kyle and grinned. "I can't believe you got the job!"

They tell us who is talking.

- "This has conk rot," a logger yelled from the top of a tree. "It's no good. Check the others" (We see who's talking, where he's at, and his yelling injects emotion.).
- "I've been away at school for some time." Becca glanced out the window (We know who's talking, that there is a window, and possibly she's uncomfortable because she's looking away, not making eye contact.).

They give us information on the setting.

- "Soon as I get the horses and stage put away." Josh climbed back in the driver's seat (We know we are in a historical setting).
- Maggie pulled out a chair for her at the kitchen table. "I have some biscuits from breakfast and some of last year's strawberry preserves left still. There's coffee, or I could make you tea if that'd sit better" (We know we are in a very homey kitchen.).

Whenever you can, make your action beats do double or triple duty. Go beyond who's talking. Let the action show us where we are, the character's emotions, and state of mind.

Subtext: How to say it without saying it

The real story is often underneath whatever is being said, and you ignore that at your peril. As Lisa Cron, author of *Story Genius* says, "Story isn't about what we do, it's about **why** we do it. It's not about what we say out loud, it's about **what we're really thinking** when we say it."

Use actions to reveal what the characters are really saying, despite their words to the contrary.

- "I have all the time in the world." Kim tapped her foot.
- "Yes, I'm fine." She looked away and pulled at her skirt.

Brandilyn Collins's *Getting Into Character* is excellent for understanding this.

This is another area where you can introduce conflict in dialogue. The hero is saying one thing but thinking another. That can provide internal conflict, which is emotionally powerful. Additionally, the antagonist can say perfectly harmless words, but his inflection and body language can imply a threat.

Interior monologue: What are you thinking?

Interior monologue is when we climb into our character's head as if we were in there too. This is how we convey to the readers what our character thinks, sees, feels as if we are thinking, seeing, and feeling it right along with them.

One of the best ways to deepen your character is by using interior monologue to get inside his head—showing us his naked thoughts. Interior monologue has risks. If you are not careful, you may wind up Telling when you should be Showing. We talked about this when we talked about Reaction scenes. Make sure that all interior monologue comes from deep POV. Make sure you are in their head, not just telling us what they are thinking and feeling.

But the rewards are great. Careful use of interior monologue can create the illusion that your reader is your character. Which is the goal we are striving for.

It is tempting to use it in long uninterrupted sequences when a character is alone and trying to figure out what to do next. An effective strategy is to work it in small lumps during your Action scenes. Interior monologue can be used more in Reaction scenes, which have a slower pace than Action scenes. A Reaction scene will often demand some internal reflection, especially during the Dilemma phase, and if the character is alone, then there is nobody else to bounce ideas off of, so the character is forced to use interior monologue.

This is a scene early in *Coming Home,* Seth's reaction to Becca's arrival.

Seth caught himself for the third time this morning looking out of the barn toward the boardinghouse. He was hoping to catch a glimpse of Becca. How was she holding up after yesterday? He didn't really need to worry; Maggie was there, and mothering people was what she lived for. Not that Becca ever needed much mothering. Still his new sense of responsibility weighed on him.

He pulled a harness down and methodically ran his hands over it, checking for cuts and tears in the leather. Though he'd been in logging for years, he helped Josh out with the stage when needed. Plus, Owen Taylor ran things just fine when Seth was gone. Maybe too fine considering he'd discovered the faulty chain. Seth shoved those thoughts away. Today the solitude of animals and the quiet, familiar barn work made a nice change from the noisy camp.

Action is interspersed with the thoughts. We can picture where Seth is, what his emotional state is, and we get a bit of backstory added for good measure.

Apply it!

- Write dialogue for an Action scene
- Write dialogue for a Reaction scene
- Write a scene with interior monologue. Then rewrite it as dialogue. Which works better? Or is it a combination of both?
- Go back to any exercise above and look at your dialogue tags. Can you make them do double or triple duty?

Chapter 12

DEEP POINT OF VIEW

THE BEST BOOKS have emotionally compelling characters, to such an extent that the readers identify with the hero and feel the same emotions as the hero. To accomplish that, you as the writer have to put the reader inside the hero's skin and have us view the world from behind her eyes. This is our point of view character. We are in her POV.

I've mentioned this before, but it is so important, it bears repeating.

One POV per scene

If you use more than one POV per scene, it is called head hopping. It doesn't create an emotional experience. When you maintain one POV per scene, it allows the reader to fully get into the character's skin. If you yank the reader out of that and pop them into another character, it gets confusing. And generally it means you have not used deep POV but something closer to omniscient.

I can't read your mind

We can only know in that scene what that POV character knows. No, "Little did she know..." Or "Soon she would find out..." Or "Looking back later, she would realize." These are signs of omniscience which pulls us into an out of body experience looking down. Not fun unless you're a ghost.

What I find is that because we watch TV and movies, we muddle POV. When you watch a TV show or a movie, they are showing you the person's face as they talk or react. When the director wants us to know what the heroine is feeling, he shows us her face, actions, and dialogue.

So often I'll see something like this:

"I cheated on the test." Mary confessed, wringing her hands. She felt awful about it. How could she make it right?

"I can't believe that," Mr. White replied. Mary was his best student. What was the world coming to if his best student cheated?

First we are in Mary's head. We know this because we hear her internal monologue. Then we are in Mr. White's head because we hear his interior monologue. This doesn't let us actually *be* in either of their skins and denies the reader an emotionally compelling experience.

Instead, it should be written like this:

"I cheated on the test." Mary confessed, wringing her hands. She felt awful about it. How could she make it right?

"I can't believe that." Mr. White shook his head and frowned.

Clearly he was disappointed in her. That made two of them. She was disappointed in herself.

We stay in Mary's head the whole time so we can more deeply feel her emotions. The same scene could also be written from Mr. White's POV depending on the goal of your scene, which you determine in your pre-writing. Additionally, you can write the same scene from different POVs to see which gives the greatest emotional experience.

Writing is very different from video. We need to crawl inside the hero's skin. When we do that, we don't see their eyes or their faces. Put yourself in the scene as your character. What are you thinking, feeling? What are you doing with your body? What things are your five senses picking up? Show us what it's like to be that person from deep inside of them, not by showing us from the outside.

As writers, we have more tools than directors do. We have access to the character's thoughts and feelings. So let's make good use of those tools.

POV don'ts:

- Don't tell us what the POV character doesn't notice.
- Don't tell us what takes place somewhere else.
- Don't tell us what will happen in the future.
- Don't tell us anything other than what the POV character is thinking and feeling at that moment.
- Don't tell us that the POV character is thinking; simply state the thought.

POV do's:

- Do know which things your POV character will notice and care about (personality, job, hobby, gender, past experience all filter this).
- Do know how your POV character will react to the situation they are in.
- Do use senses to reflect your POV character's experience in the world (sight, sound, smell, taste, touch).
- Do establish whose POV we are in at the beginning of the scene.

In each scene, we need to have a POV character. That may be the hero or it may be someone else. How do you determine who should be the POV character of the scene? Generally it is the person in the scene with the most to lose. It could also be the person with the greatest emotional response, which may or may not be the same person.

Once we know whose scene it is, we need to make sure that we write it from deep POV. That is, from inside the mind, skin, and behind the eyes of the POV character.

Words that indicate you may be breaking deep POV are:

- Think/thought
- Ponder
- Realize
- Wonder
- Understand
- Reflect
- Consider
- Muse

- Deliberate
- Ask himself/herself
- Felt
- Know/knew
- Sense
- Decide

Senses

One of the best ways to let us know that we are in the hero's skin is through the senses. When you are editing a scene, think a moment about what information all five senses are giving your POV character. Sight and touch are easy and the most overused. But what about smell and taste? You can pull on deep emotions with those. They often evoke strong memories, and you can use that to your advantage. Don't forget about hearing too.

However, you don't want a laundry list of all the senses. When you are taking stock, think about which two senses will evoke the greatest emotional experience for your reader. Where in the scene would be the best place to put those senses? Where would they evoke the strongest reaction?

The key is not to just include the senses for the sake of it. But to give them to the reader as a clue as to how the hero is feeling. It all comes back to feelings. The more we know what the hero is feeling, the more we can relate and feel like we are there and in her skin.

Warning: Only include things the character can see, hear, touch, taste, and smell. Don't write "if only she knew what was waiting for her around the corner." She can't see it, so she doesn't know about it. Neither do we. "She didn't notice the car following her." If she didn't notice it, neither did we. That's breaking POV.

Even if she can see it, do you need to include it? If you

tell us about something, we are going to think it's important and relevant. So only mention the book on the sidewalk if it's going to be important or if it's important that your character noticed it. This goes back to the brain only wanting information that is relevant.

Now, what does your character do with this information? Sometimes it's enough to mention the smell of Mom's apple pie. But what about a math book laying open on the sidewalk in front of the house? What does your hero think about that? What does she think it means? Is she confused, scared, mad, happy? How would your hero view it differently than other characters? The *interpretation* of the sense stimulus is just as important the stimulus itself.

Writing emotion follows naturally from writing about the senses because the senses often trigger emotions. And we need to treat writing about them the same way.

Like with any writing exercise, the first step is to just write and be in your creative brain. Then when you've had time to let it sit, go back with the editor brain. Be as concrete and descriptive as you can be. Go over every adverb. Can you make the verb stronger? Can you say it in a fresh way?

Show, don't tell

The main thing to remember is to show us that your character is angry instead of telling us. Get us into your POV character's skin and let us experience the emotion from behind her eyes.

From our earlier example in *Coming Home*.

> Seth gave him a terse nod and strode out the door, rounding the building and heading for the outhouse. He stared at it for a moment before hauling back and slamming his fist into the door.

Not once did I say that Seth was angry. But you can see that he is.

But sometimes you do want to tell. A great tip I heard was, "Show the important parts. Tell the boring parts." And that makes sense. Telling is faster, and you can cover a lot of ground that you may only need to mention to get from point A to point B.

Also remember, the brain is searching for relevant information. It's trying to thrive and survive, and so it's looking for information on how to do that. If you Show everything, even things that aren't relevant to the Story Goal or Internal Goal, the brain will get overloaded and stop trusting the author.

Apply it!

- Go to your previously written scenes and rewrite from another character's POV. How does that change the scene? Does it make it more emotionally compelling? Or less?
- Look at the list of words that indicate you might be breaking deep POV. Are you using any of them? Can you make the POV deeper?
- What senses are you using in these scenes? Can you evoke even stronger emotions with a different sense?

Chapter 13

AVOIDING WRITER'S BLOCK

WE HAVE ARRIVED at the last chapter. Yay! We've worked through the Novel Blueprint and given you all the building blocks you need to construct your novel. The rest will just take practice. But I still have a few tips that you might find useful.

Creative brain versus the editing brain

We have touched on all the structure and techniques you need to write your novel. Now, I'm going to veer a little bit into the editing process. You won't want to go crazy with editing while you're on your first draft, but if you're like me, your fingers will be itching to make changes. Here's how to do that without giving yourself a case of writer's block.

Separate writing and editing

Writing and editing are two different parts of the brain. When you are writing, you need to resist the urge to critique or change any actual writing at this point. You want to stay in creative or writing brain to keep the ideas flowing. Jot things down now. Fix things later. I've mentioned how I use the Document Notes section of Scrivener to keep track of these types of things so I can keep writing. Whatever method you use, create a place to put those niggling thoughts so your creative brain can get back to creating without interference.

When you are done creating, put your work aside and come back to it later. A little distance is a great thing. I usually start each writing session reading over what I wrote last time, making changes to satisfy my editor brain. I've had usually a day's break from the writing, so I can see things a bit more clearly. Now I can come back with the editor brain and start applying structure and analyze and fix things.

Then when I get into my new writing, my editor brain is satisfied that the system works and nothing will be forgotten. Don't mix up the editor and creative brain or you will get yourself stuck with writer's block.

There are a few areas that you might want to look at while you are in your editing brain.

Grammar, spelling, etc.

Definitely check for these things when you are in editing mode. Learn about what you don't know and what you need to know. Take an online class if you need to. Read your work out loud or have a program read to you. It will catch the things your eyes will skip right over. Print out a copy and edit there. Your brain will see different things in different formats. When you get to that all-important final draft, get proofreaders and editors and beta readers, preferably people who are looking at your work with fresh eyes.

How to avoid writer's block

Okay, now that we've covered the topics we need to look out for during our editing sessions, let's circle back to the creative brain and the dreaded writer's block. You want to write but the words just won't come. Why? And how to fix it?

Writer's block is caused, usually, by two things. One, mixing the Creative Brain with the Editing Brain. We've talked before about how you have to shut off your editing brain while you are writing and let your creative brain come out to play.

There are some interesting tools you can use to help with this if it's a problem. Dictation can help some people talk their story on to the page. There is software that only allows you to see a few lines of your work and one that starts eating the words you've written if you don't keep typing. Talk about pressure!

This is also the theory behind National Novel Writing Month (NaNoWriMo) in November. It's the idea that having a deadline to write a book in a month will spur you on to just put words on the page and not worry about editing them. This can work if you have a plan like the Novel Blueprint and aren't just roaming about aimlessly.

The process of turning off your editor takes a bit of training, but your brain can get better at it with time. Just keep reminding yourself that you can fix it later. Even if you literally write those words in your manuscript.

The other cause of writer's block is Blank Page Syndrome. That's when you are staring at a blank page and have no idea what to write. Now, doing all the work we've done up to this point, you're not too likely to have this problem. But you might have a few places where you're just not sure how a scene should go. The best solution I've found for this is prewriting.

I've mentioned this before, but prewriting is one of the best ways to beat writer's block and to ensure that your scene has all of the great components it needs before you even get writing it. It's also a way to write more quickly, because when you know what a scene is going to be about, it's easier to see it play out in your head and then you are nearly transcribing what you are seeing.

Before I write a scene, I make some notes in the Document Notes section of my scene in Scrivener. Here are the questions I want to answer before I write the scene:

- Whose POV is it?
- What is their goal for this scene? How can I create obstacles or disasters for that?
- Who else might be in the scene or needs to be in the scene?
- Is this an Action scene or a Reaction scene?
- What could be some of the Goal/Conflict/Disaster (Action scene) or the Reaction/Dilemma/Decision (Reaction scene)?
- What's come before that needs to be addressed, like a decision or a disaster?
- What are we heading toward next that we need to be setting up now?
- How does this go to the emotional wound/lie of the POV character?
- Sketch out how the dialogue might go. What is each person's agenda? Subtext? Body language?

As you can see, by starting to ask these questions, you move right into creative brain, drawing on all the work you've already done. It ensures that you are writing relevant scenes that pull the reader through the story and create an emotional experience.

Congratulations!

You have started on a journey many people want to take, but so few ever attempt. Even fewer finish the books they've started. And you know why now. It's hard! But you can do it. You have the tools. Here are a few other things to consider on your writing journey.

Find other writers

Even if you can't find a critique group, you can often find likeminded folks online or in person. I run a membership group for writers that, while it doesn't provide critiques, does provide that kind of camaraderie and accountability you can find in a traditional critique group. For more information, see the Resources section next.

Keep learning

Read books, attend conferences, take classes. All of these will help you in some way or another become a better writer. There is a saying that leaders are learners. Well writers are learners too. Never stop trying to learn and perfect your craft. See the Resources section for more about the classes I teach.

Now go forth and write!

Chapter 14

RESOURCES

BOOKS ON CRAFT

Angela Ackerman and Becca Puglisi, *The Emotion Thesaurus*

Blake Snyder, *Save the Cat*

Brandilyn Collins, *Getting Into Character*

Christopher Vogler, *The Writer's Journey: Mythic Structure for Writers*

Donald Maas, *Writing the Breakout Novel Workbook*

Dwight Swain *Techniques of the Selling Writer*

James Scott Bell, *Plot & Structure*

Jeff Gerke, *Plot Versus Character*

Jen Crosswhite, *Posts from the Pencildancers: Short Bites to Improve Your Writing Today*

Lisa Cron, *Story Genius* and *Wired for Story*

Randy Ingermanson's Advanced Fiction Writing e-zine

Randy Ingermanson, *How to Write a Dynamite Scene Using the Snowflake Method*

Rayne Hall, *Writing Deep Point of View*

Renni Browne and Dave King, *Self-Editing for Fiction Writers*

Sol Stein, *Stein on Writing*

Susan May Warren, *Deep and Wide* and *The Story Equation* and *From the Inside Out: Discover, Create, and Polish the Novel in You*

OTHER BOOKS

David Keirsey, *Please Understand Me II* and *Sixteen Types*

Gary Chapman, *The Five Love Languages*

Ian Morgan Cron, *The Road Back To You*

John Eldredge, *Wild at Heart*

John and Staci Eldredge, *Captivating*

Malcolm Gladwell, *Outliers*

Suzanne Stabile, *The Path Between Us*

SOFTWARE AND WEBSITES

Scrivener

Toggl.com

Tandem Services Ink (This is my site where I offer a membership site for writers and my classes. Sign up for more information.)

Margie Lawson's classes

en.wikipedia.org/wiki/Enneagram_of_Personality

www.enneagraminstitute.com

www.9types.com

similarminds.com/test.html free test (I haven't taken it yet, so proceed at your own risk).

Basic character chart: Basic questions to ask about your characters

- What's the best thing that can happen to the hero?
- What's the worst?
- What decision does the hero have to make?
- What does hero have to lose?
- What does hero have to gain? (The stakes have to be high enough for us to care)
- What needs to change about the hero? Where do they need to grow? What's their blind spot?
- What do they miss by not changing?
- What event forces them to change or to choose to change?
- How do they try to cheat? By not doing the work required for growth but taking a short cut. How does that make things worse?
- What are their finances like?
- What is their biggest fear?
- What is their biggest secret?
- What is their blind spot?
- How do others see them?
- How do they see themselves?
- What is the lie they believe?
- What is the truth that sets them free?
- List their flaws and strengths, bad habits
- List their hopes/dreams
- What are their secrets? (leads to conflict)
- Body language: tells, tics, habits, gestures, mannerisms
- Physical Description: height, weight, age, gender, body type, tattoos, piercings, distinguishing

features. Favorite body part, most hated body part. Illness or disability.

- Background/environment
- Hobbies and interests, entertainment
- Career
- Talents, skills, super powers, abilities
- Education
- Friends
- Enemies
- Favorite food/dessert/drink
- Belief system (religious, political, social)
- Life history: family background, happy and traumatic childhood events
- Relationship status and history
- What makes her angry? How does she handle anger?
- What makes her embarrassed? How does she handle embarrassment?
- Who is her hero? Who does she admire? Why?
- How has your character been deceived?

Faith questions to ask your character:

- Does he believe?
- Has he ever believed?
- Why doesn't he believe?
- What made him lose faith in the Lord?
- When did he practice his faith?
- What makes him turn to God for help?
- When did he give himself to Christ? Why?
- How does he practice his faith?
- Does he have doubts about his faith? Why?
- How does his faith help him when he falters?
- What kind of temptations has he dealt with?

- What kind of questions does he have about God?
- What kind of faith does his family have?

Writer's Conferences

In the past, I've had a couple of questions that are a bit beyond the scope of this book, but I'll touch on them here to get you headed in the right direction.

As I mentioned earlier, it's important to have the support of other writers on this journey. One way to find that is at writer's conferences. If you write in a particular genre, there is likely a writer's group for that genre, and they likely have a national conference. ACFW, RWA, Mystery Writers of America, SciFi writers, Thrillerfest, these are all big name shows.

These genre-based groups also often have local or regional chapters that put on their own conferences. If one is near you, that can be a great option, and you might make friends with someone you could physically meet up with on occasion.

There are also regional conferences that are just for writers of any genre or nonfiction. These can also be great options and generally are more budget friendly.

The best way to find them is to keep your ears open to where other writers are going, and you can also Google writer's conferences. There are many top lists out there that can get you pointed in the right direction.

The advantage of a national conference is they pull in big-name publishers, agents, and speakers. You can learn a lot, and if one of those publishers or agents is on your wish list, it's a great way to try to meet them. You can also network with other authors and learn a lot about craft, marketing, and the industry in general. Most all publishers and many agents don't take unsolicited manuscripts. Which means you can't just send them your work and expect them to read it. You have to have an invitation or a request. And you can get that at a writer's conference.

For regional conferences, their big advantage is the cost and the time. They are closer, cheaper, and often don't run as long as the national conferences. And everybody has to live somewhere. Your dream agent or publisher might live close enough to be part of a regional conference. Additionally, lot of people who aren't big names can still give you a ton of value. So don't overlook that, even if you don't recognize their name.

The biggest advantage of all conferences is getting to hang out with other writers. These are people who think like you do and who "get" you. It's just refreshing to talk shop and not have to explain yourself. Plus, I've developed several life-long friendships from conferences. And you never know what business connections you might make.

The cons are that national conferences are expensive. I've spent at least $10,000 on conferences in my writing career. They take up a lot of time too. They can go as long as five days. Also, you're competing with other writers for time with agents, editors, etc. There's no guarantee that an agent or editor will want your manuscript or even look at it.

And there's no real chance to get an evaluation of your work. You might be able to get a critique if they offer it. Usually it's paid, and only about ten to thirty pages. So it's hard to know how to really move forward with your writing craft.

It all goes back to your why. If you are looking for (ahem, stalking) a particular editor or agent, then it might be worth it for you to go wherever they are. If there is a particular learning track they are offering that you are interested in, that can also be helpful.

If you want to meet other writers, a local or regional conference might be a better bet. If you want feedback on your work, you'd be better off hiring an editor or a writing coach, probably for less money.

Agents

You really can't get very far in the traditional publishing world without an agent. Most publishing houses won't look at a manuscript without an agent. And even if they did, the contracts are skewed heavily in their favor, not yours.

But agents can be as hard to find as publishing houses. You can approach them in basically two ways: a conference or by query letter.

This is really the main advantage of conferences, especially big ones. You can meet agents. Sometimes they take appointments, sometimes they have a table at meals. In any situation, there is an opportunity to find out what they are looking for and to talk to them about your work. There is something to be said about meeting someone in person and putting a face and a name with a project versus something that just comes in via email. It's much more personal and your chances definitely increase. Plus, the fact that you're at a conference shows that you are dedicated to your work and are treating it like a professional.

If you can't get to a conference or the agent you want isn't attending any, you can send a query letter. That's beyond the scope of this class, but you can Google query letters and get some solid advice. Make sure you check the agency's website, spell everyone's name correctly, and only send them what they ask. It can take a long time to hear back from an agent, but usually they have guidelines on when they respond by. It's appropriate to make a gentle inquiry after that time, but after that, assume they aren't interested and move on.

Some agents focus primarily on getting your manuscript in front of acquisitions editors and shepherding it through the publication process, advocating for you. Remember though, agents have working relationships with these editors that they rely on, so they're not likely to burn any bridges going to bat for you. Consider them more of a mediator.

Some agents also offer career coaching and guidance. Some will edit your books in house first or send you to an editor. Some will help you brainstorm your next book or series. Depending on what you want or need, make sure you are clear on your expectations and what they are going to deliver for you.

Afterword

Thanks for joining me on this journey through the Novel Blueprint.

Hungry for more? Join the Tandem Services membership site—Craft. Career. Commerce. Community—take one of our writing courses where we go much deeper into these topics.

Be informed of the latest information by signing up for our Craft. Career. Community. Community updates at http://tandem-services.ck.page/e18b9f7bf7 so you'll be the first to know about the latest releases of courses and books. Your email address will never be shared, and you can unsubscribe at any time.

If you enjoyed this book, please leave a review. Reviews can be as simple as "I couldn't put it down. I can't wait for the next one" and help raise the author's visibility and lets other readers find her.

Acknowledgments

Great thanks to Tracy Borgmeyer for being my very first guinea pig and helping me nail down the stimulus/response terminology. And to my students who have let me work out these ideas on them and given me their feedback.

Much love to Diana Lesire Brandmeyer and Jennifer Lynn Cary for the mad-rush read through. You guys are the best!

And to Morgan Gist MacDonald of Paper Raven Books. I'm so glad we connected all those years ago. You push me to do bigger and better things, and I love it!

Much thanks and love to my children, Caitlyn Elizabeth and Joshua Alexander, for supporting my dream for many years and giving me time to write. And most of all to my Lord Jesus, who makes all things possible and directs my paths.

About the Author

Jen Crosswhite is owner and proprietor of Tandem Services.

A California native who's spent significant time in the Midwest, she has over fifteen years of experience in business, marketing, and publishing. Over this time, she has held the titles of marketing director, managing editor, and director of communication.

She is a bestselling author, having ghost-written nonfiction and written novels, curriculum, and award-winning articles and short stories.

Her passion is to help other authors improve their craft, develop their writing careers, find community within her membership site, and create effective commerce around their books.

She partners with other industry experts to create a team that will provide you with the best product possible.

www.TandemServicesInk.com
Twitter: @jenlcross
Facebook: Tandem Services
Instagram: jencrosswhite
Pinterest: Author Jennifer Crosswhite

facebook.com/tandemservicescreative

twitter.com/jenlcross

instagram.com/jencrosswhite

pinterest.com/jtiszai

Also by Jen Crosswhite

Nonfiction

Posts from the Pencildancers: Short bites to improve your writing today

Eat the Elephant: How to write your novel one bite at a time

Contemporary Romance

The Inn at Cherry Blossom Lane

Can the summer magic of Lake Michigan bring first loves back together? Or will the secret they discover threaten everything they love?

Historical Romance

The Route Home Series

Be Mine

A woman searching for independence. A man searching for education. Can a simple thank you note turn into something more?

Coming Home

He was why she left. Now she's falling for him. Can a woman who turned her back on her hometown come home to find justice for her brother without falling in love with his best friend?

The Road Home

He is a stagecoach driver just trying to do his job. She is returning to her suitor only to find he has died. When a stack of stolen money shows up in her bag, she thinks the past she has desperately tried to hide has come back to haunt her.

Books by JL Crosswhite

Romantic Suspense

The Hometown Heroes Series

Promise Me

Cait can't catch a break. What she witnessed could cost her job and her beloved farmhouse. Will Greyson help her or only make things worse?

Protective Custody

She's a key witness in a crime shaking the roots of the town's power brokers. He's protecting a woman he'll risk everything for. Doing the right thing may cost her everything. Including her life.

Flash Point

She's a directionally-challenged architect who stumbled on a crime that could destroy her life's work. He's a firefighter protecting his hometown… and the woman he loves.

Special Assignment

A brain-injured Navy pilot must work with the woman in charge of the program he blames for his injury. As they both grasp to save their careers, will their growing attraction hinder them as they attempt solve the mystery of who's really at fault before someone else dies?

Made in the USA
Columbia, SC
07 February 2020